Wallace-Homestead

PRICE·GUIDE·TO
BASKETS

FRANCES THOMPSON-JOHNSON

To
Kim Johnson

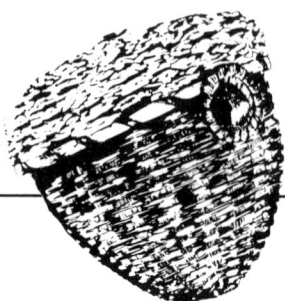

Cover design: Anthony Jacobson
Interior layout: Anthony Jacobson
Editor: Stephen Levy

Library of Congress Catalog Card Number 87-50294

ISBN 0-87069-489-8

Copyright 1987, Wallace-Homestead Book Company.
All rights reserved.

No part of this publication may be reproduced, stored in a retrieval system, or transmitted in any form or by any means—electronic, mechanical, photocopying, recording, or otherwise—without prior permission of the publisher.

10 9 8 7 6 5 4 3 2 1

Published by

A Capital Cities/ABC, Inc. Company

Wallace-Homestead Book Company
Post Office Box 5406
Greensboro, NC 27403
(919) 275-9809

Acknowledgments

Thanks to all the people who shared basket information and allowed me to photograph their collections, and a special thanks to the following who went that extra mile to share: Linda Farve, Philadelphia, MS; Faye Stouff, Jeanerette, LA; Susie Sylestine and Marian John, Elton, LA; The Peter Smith Terry Basket Collection, Dr. Chris Marshall, and Unity College, Unity, Maine; Ralph Bishop, Troy, Maine; Phill McIntrye and Daughters, and Barlow's Antiques, Anson, Maine; George Morrill Auctions, Gray, Maine; Miccosukee Indian Village, Miami, FL; Regina Hines, Ball Ground, GA; John Coker,

New Market, TN; Maryann Sklar, Newport, TN; Caroline French and Parker-French Antique Center, Northwood, NH; Anne Chester, Window Rock, AZ; Dr. Ann Bailey, Tucson, AZ; Basketville, Putney, VT; Lightner Museum, St. Augustine, FL; Thomas J. Sabiston, U. S. Army Aviation Museum, Ft. Rucker, AL; Blount Museum, Knoxville, TN; Old World Importers, Columbus, Ohio; Pike Museum, Troy, AL; Jan P. Christman, The Shaker Museum, Old Chatham, NY; Jon and Carla Magoun, South Paris, Maine; Arundel Antique Village, Kennebunkport, Maine; Chief To-Me-Kin, Wells, Maine; Ms. Zundel, Harry and David, Medford, Oregon; Doug Fernald, Penobscot Indian Museum, Rosalie Clark, and Eunice Crawley, Old Town Maine; Stephen Zeh, Temple, Maine; Ron and Anne Riendeau Auctions, Topsham, Maine; Mary Vanderhorst, Mt. Pleasant, SC; and Carolyn Jones, Country Place Antiques, Graceville, FL.

Contents

Dedication .... *ii*

Acknowledgments .... *iii*

Introduction 1

Basketry from A to Z 5

Introduction

There is a tendency to call any container with a handle a basket, and any without a handle a box. The dictionary describes a basket as "a container made of interwoven materials such as rushes, twigs, and strips of wood." No mention is made of a handle—just a container.

Accepting this on face value is very fortunate, indeed, since our ancestors made some very interesting containers of interwoven rushes, twigs, strips of wood, and grasses. By accepting the container theory, a whole new world of collecting is opened to us.

The use of woven or basketry items

goes back to ancient times. Early civilizations used woven basketry items for all their needs; there were no other containers at the time. Indians used basketry to make everything from canoes to containers for food and water, long before the European settlers arrived.

The Pilgrims

We know that basketry was an accepted craft for the Pilgrims and had been for a long time before they even set sail for the New World. Basketmaking was well enough established to warrant a basketmakers guild in England as early as 1569. The guild was designed to protect the users of baskets—as a sort of weight and measurement inspection. Since goods were often purchased by the peck or bushel, and the only means of measurement were the baskets, it was important for a basket to hold a full measure. Thus, the guild was organized and commissioned to check baskets in the same way the scale at the fruit market is checked for accuracy. If a basket was found to be undersize, it was confiscated and burned.

The Pilgrims brought this feeling of fair play with them to the New World. Once here, they exchanged basketmaking ideas with the Indians. By combining methods, both the Indians and Pilgrims probably each ended up using the best and easiest methods.

Old records show the importance of baskets in the lives of the early settlers and how much they treasured them. In fact, they valued baskets enough to mention them in their wills and inventories. Several inventories of the 1600s list winnowing baskets, as well as bushel and half-bushel baskets.

Early Settlers

The early settlers were also known to have made weirs (fish and eel traps), as well as cradles for the newborns. All of these were woven of various materials. After all, there were no paper bags or boxes, no plastic containers, not even tin containers for those early settlers.

Americans have never lost their love of basketry. After containers of other types became available, they continued to make baskets. Not as many as before, perhaps, but now they had time to experiment with miniatures and novelties.

Later, Americans began to use basketry techniques to make furniture—wicker furniture. Originally, this furniture was called basket furniture; only in recent years has that name changed to wicker.

Incidentally, *basketry* is defined as the craft or process of making baskets; or, it may be used to describe baskets collectively.

The Rebirth of Basketry

Through the years, the popularity of baskets has experienced many highs and lows. Perhaps the biggest lull in basketmaking came right after World War II when new inventions and materials began flooding the market. The country was slowly changing and there was little or no demand for baskets, not even old ones.

This changed drastically, however, a decade or so ago when basketmaking and collecting reached a new high. Never before had there been so many people making, selling, and teaching basketry. As it has always been, the fascination for basketmaking appeals to both men and women; yet recently, there has been a surprising amount of interest in basketmaking by business executives who have learned to make baskets for its relaxation value. Others have gone into it as a profession, making baskets to sell to a basket-loving public.

Classes in basketry are very popular both at local colleges and on Indian reservations. Current prices for baskets, both old and new, has encouraged many young women to enroll in basketry classes. Not only do these new basketmakers enjoy the satisfaction of creating baskets, it's inexpensive and the actual basketmaking process is both rewarding and relaxing.

For the past several years it has been rare to find a magazine that doesn't include pictures that show baskets in them—usually in room decorations. And it's refreshing to find frequent articles in local newspapers describing the accomplishments of local individuals involved in basketmaking. Basketmaking has never had so many devotees.

Using This Book

Baskets are handmade, which means that each one will be somewhat different from all others. Thus, it's almost impossible to find two that are identical in every way. The size of baskets can be even more misleading in photos: For instance, a close-up lens can make the smallest basket look like a cotton basket. For that reason, this book includes measurements for many of the baskets illustrated (measurements are to the nearest quarter inch). In addition, each picture caption has a letter(s) or description as follows:

h	height
o.h.	overall height, including the handle
l	length
w	width
dia	diameter at the widest point

About Prices

Trying to pin down an exact price on anything can be difficult. The same item is often priced differently from one store to another. This price difference is especially true for items that aren't new.

The prices in this book are intended as a guide and are based on actual prices paid, or the prices asked, for baskets around the country. As a general rule, baskets are less expensive in New England because they are more plentiful. In this case, plentiful refers to the old Indian-made ash-splint and sweet-grass baskets made in the area.

The price of new baskets varies from one maker to another, but the prices given in this book are the exact asking prices that were given to the author at the time the author visited each facility.

Another factor affecting the price of baskets is popularity. A type of basket that may be popular in one part of the country may not be in another. An example is the oak-splint baskets made in the mountain states. They're bringing unbelievable prices in those areas, yet in New England the swing handle is more popular, especially those made of ash splints.

The best advice is that you should not buy a basket you feel is overpriced until you have looked in many antique shops, shows, and malls. Some dealers are better buyers than others, and can and do buy and sell for less. Unless it is a basket you have been searching for, for a long time, or one so rare you don't know when you'll see another, take a little time to think it over.

Below each basket pictured is a description of the basket. Following the description is the price, and then the place it was found along with the type of outlet—shop, mall, show, or auction. Last, the date or year the item was found is listed. A few of the photos were made in museums or private collections and it was impossible to get current prices. In that case, the name of the place where the basket was found and NPA (no price available) are listed.

Basketry from A to Z

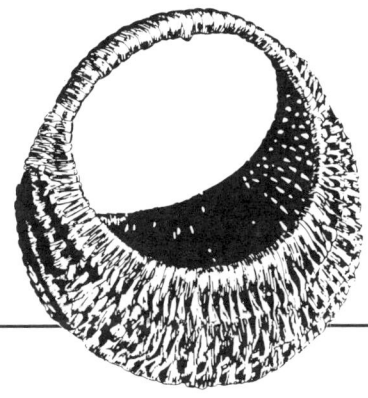

Abenaki Indians

Although the Abenaki Indians lived on the reservation on the St. Francis River in Quebec, they spent their summers from 1870 through 1920 in the resort towns of Old Forge, Saratoga Lake, Lake Mahopak, and Lake George, New York; Ottawa Beach, Michigan; Asbury Park and Atlantic City, New Jersey; and the White Mountains of New Hampshire. They were there making and selling baskets.

In the winter they worked at home making baskets to sell at the resorts during the summer. According to reports, some of the more popular makers couldn't keep up with the demand, and therefore hired others who only wanted to work summers. The Abenakis rented houses and shops in and near the resort areas where they established their businesses—making and selling baskets.

Meanwhile, other basketmakers, who preferred to stay home on the reservation in the summer, worked for the large wholesalers who found such a demand for the baskets that they mailed out catalogues.

Many of the basketmakers who worked the resort areas reported making between $4,000 and $5,000 a year, not a measly amount for those times.

The basketmakers living in New England might not have been as involved as the Abenakis, but they were in the middle of the tourist areas and could stay home with their roadside stands as well as do contract work for the Shakers. When the basket production all over the country is combined for this period, it's easy to see why there are still so many baskets and basketry items available to the collector.

Wall-hanging basket, type made by the Abenakis. 4½" w, 11" l, 9" h. $65, New York antique shop, 1986.

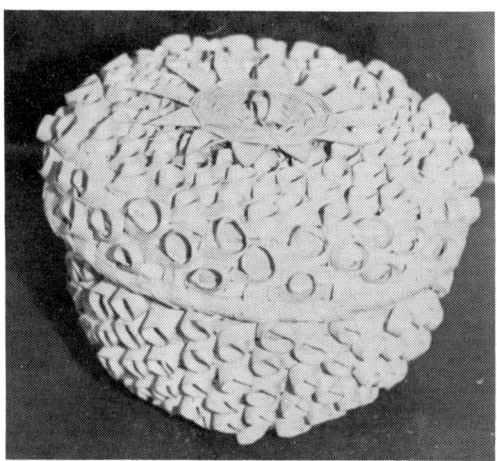

Covered basket, ash splint, souvenir type, Unity College collection, NPA.

Fancy ash-splint basket. 4" dia, 4½" h. $25, Maine antique show, 1987.

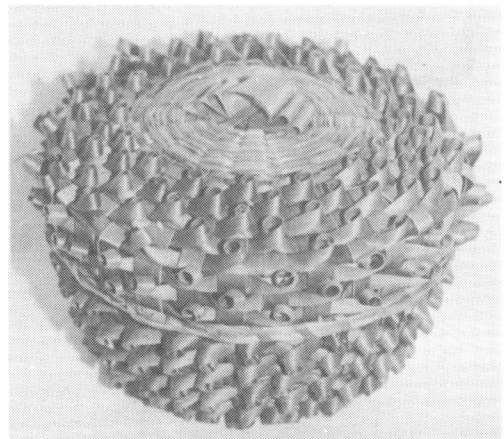

Another style of souvenir basket, ash splint, Unity College collection, NPA.

Acorn Picking-and-Storing Baskets

Customs varied with each tribe of Indian, and of course, their locations influenced customs to a degree. But regardless of location or custom, there was only one acorn harvest per year; therefore, the acorns had to be gathered and stored as quickly as possible. The men and boys climbed the trees and shook them to make acorns fall so the women and children could pick them up.

Some tribes designed their own acorn scoops, or nut scoops, so the acorns could be picked up with as little effort as possible; others continued to crawl around on the ground, picking up the nuts a few at a time.

Once the acorns were gathered, it was the women's chore to transform the bitter acorn into tasty food—a chore in which they were well skilled. Nevertheless, it was a long and tiring one. First, the acorns had to be shelled. This required cracking the shells gently, and then picking out the kernels. Two baskets were required for this job: the picking-and-storing basket and another for the shelled kernels. Then, using crude apparatus resembling a mortar and pestle, the women ground the acorns into meal. To remove the tannin that not only made a very bitter taste but was considered dangerous to one's health if too much was consumed, they would dig a hole in the sand, pack acorn meal around the sides, and then pour hot water over the meal until most of the tannin was gone. Finally, the acorn meal was ready to be made into bread or soup.

Cherokees may have used this basket for storing acorns or meal. River-cane covered basket, private collection, NPA.

Acorn Scoop

An acorn scoop was a handled affair with a loosely woven bottom that could be run along the ground to pick up acorns or nuts. The user could shake it to remove as much dirt and leaves as possible before putting the acorns in the basket.

Acorn-Shaped Basket

For many years, acorns played a strong role in the survival of the Indians. In the early years, despite the bitter taste, acorns were one of the staple foods. When the Indians, especially those in the Northeast, began making items for the tourist trade, they designed and made basketry items that resembled things they saw daily—things that

Depending on location and tribe, this elm basket may have been used for gathering. 20" l, 9" w, 14" o.h. $125 damaged condition, Kentucky antique shop, 1985.

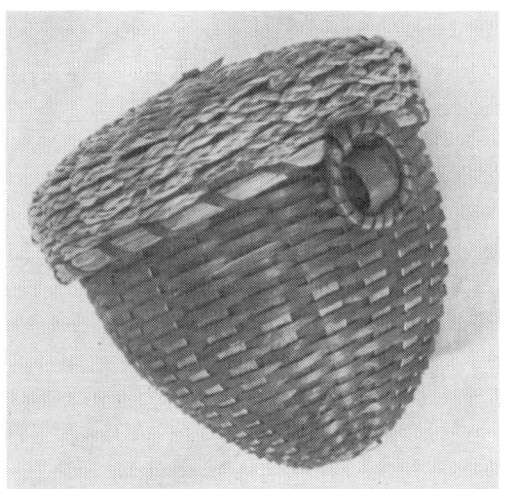

Acorn-shaped basket. 4" h, 4½" dia $35, New Hampshire Mall, fall 1986.

were familiar to them. One of the souvenir pieces was a small basket shaped like an acorn. The slightly pointed ash-splint bottom was dyed green while the sweet-grass top over ash spokes or standards was natural or brown. Credit for the design is usually given the Passamaquoddies, but more than likely, every basketmaker in the area eventually made them.

Adirondack-Type Baskets

Adirondack is a term used to describe a type of twig or branch furniture made during the first decades of this century. Rather primitive and inexpensive, it was used mostly as lawn furniture or for lake and mountain cabins. Often the bark was left on the branches, which could range in size from quite small to perhaps two inches in diameter. It's not the most attractive furniture in the world, but during the past few years it has experienced a revival in popularity. This, in turn, has sparked a revised interest in baskets made by the same method. The baskets are either used with furniture, or separately for fruit and flower arrangements.

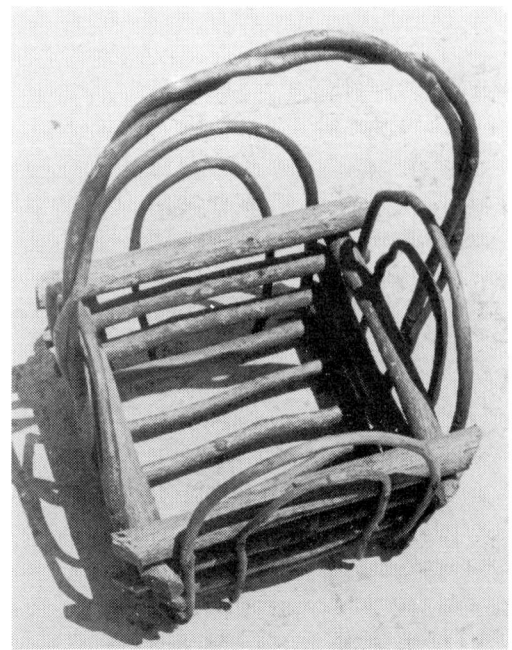

Andirondack-type basket. 12" square, 13" o.h. $25, Florida antique shop, spring 1986.

Aging New Baskets

Since an old basket is normally priced approximately ten times that of its new equivalent, it is safe to assume that there will be more aging in the future than in the past. There are those who have been looking to take advantage of this by aging baskets using different processes. This has been going on for a decade or more now, since the popularity and prices of old baskets began to soar. Rather than try to age new baskets, however, some are now opting for paint—inside and out in never-before-used colors.

It's true that some of the older baskets were painted, usually in the old red, blue, light–mustard yellow, and dark green colors. These baskets were probably painted shortly after they were made. Also, some of the old baskets were painted during the past 50 years. They were painted in order to modernize them so they could be used in different settings, rather than look like work baskets.

The new basket on the left was painted; the small one on the right was aged in New England.

During the depression there was a great surge of painting everything from furniture to baskets. Apparently, money was so scarce, it was simpler and cheaper to paint what one had rather than try to buy something new. The homemaker longing for something new in the home painted both furniture and baskets.

More often than not, older baskets were painted only on the outside. Newly painted ones, however, (seen in antique shops, shows, and malls) seem to have been spray painted in colors like dusty rose, bright yellow, and "sickly" green. They're painted inside and out, without a speck of splint showing, so that one cannot tell if the basket is old or new. This is not aging, but rather covering up the new.

Another way to age new baskets is to hang them outside so they're exposed to both rain and sun. In less than a year, oak splint baskets exposed this way in the Deep South will turn a golden brown—brown enough to pass for an old basket. In the border states of Tennessee and Kentucky, baskets turn a grayish color when left in the sun and rain. Basket-aging experiments in New England have produced a darker basket with black spots resembling mold or maybe soot.

Alaskan Baskets

Most of the Alaskan baskets are made by Eskimos living in the area. See Eskimo.

Amana Colonies

In 1842 a group of German and Swiss immigrants, fleeing their native countries to avoid further religious persecution, came to America, first stopping in New York and finally moved to Iowa around 1855. There, they acquired land and built seven self-sufficient villages for the 800 residents. Each family had an individual home, but they used a communal kitchen and dining room. Each village had its own shops—a bakery, a blacksmith, a general store, and a basketmaker. Over the years, the basketmakers made a tremendous number of baskets, most of them from willow. Some were made of peeled willow, some unpeeled, and others were a combination of both.

In 1932, the villagers voted to abandon the communal system of living, and went their separate ways in the world of free enterprise. Few baskets from this group have since been made, especially baskets for the public, but there are still a few of the old Amana-made baskets available.

American Balsam Fir

Small evergreen of the myrrh family used in basketmaking. See Balm of Gilead.

American Ivy

Another name for Virginia creeper, a vine used in basketry. See Virginia Creeper.

Anasazi

A Navajo word meaning "Ancient Ones" that is generally used now to describe the Southwest Indian basketmaker period, especially the third or last period.

Appalachian Baskets

Actually, few—if any—baskets are known strictly as Appalachian baskets; instead, they're usually referred to as baskets made in that area. Mountain people and Cherokee Indians both made a tremendous number of oak, hickory-splint, and river-cane baskets. In fact, they're still making them. Both old and newly made baskets are quite popular now, and prices are high.

Small mountain-made egg basket. $150, Tennessee auction, fall 1985.

Well-made Appalachian splint basket. $175, Tennessee auction, fall 1985.

Well-made oak-splint basket. $165, damage in bottom, Tennessee auction, fall 1985.

Round oak-splint work basket. $145, Tennessee auction, fall 1985.

The most sought after and the most expensive are the so-called "egg baskets" in the gizzard or buttocks shape. Generally, plain and serviceable baskets like the round and square work and field baskets were made, although quite a few fancy baskets—those made with splints or cane, dyed with vegetal dyes to form fancy designs—were also produced. Some makers chose to carve fancy handles on otherwise plain baskets.

Mountaineers are know for making more serviceable baskets, while the Cherokees are noted for their fancy baskets with the colorful designs. Both the settlers and Cherokees made baskets from different types of vines, but it appears that the Indians made the majority of them.

*Open Cherokee river-cane basket, approximately 50 years old. **$500**, Tennessee auction, fall 1985.*

Apple Basket

Baskets of one type or another have always been used to gather apples, whether from only a few trees or from an entire orchard. Wire baskets or factory-made wooden splint baskets have been used, as well as baskets woven to fit the needs of the pickers. Many of the fruit-gathering baskets, especially apple and peach baskets, have raised centers in order to prevent undue weight on the apples in the center. Some of the specially-made apple baskets were designed oblong with a handle on only one side. This design would allow the basket to be tipped forward so the apples could roll out slowly and easily, thereby preventing as many bruises as possible.

*One-handled oak-splint basket. 15" w, 24" l, 16" h. **$65**, Florida antique shop, fall 1986.*

*Open Cherokee river-cane basket, 50 years old. **$800**, Kentucky antique shop, spring 1986.*

*Factory-made apple picking-and-storing baskets in half and bushel sizes. **$45** and **$65**, North Carolina antique shop, fall 1986.*

Factory-made apple basket with wooden handles. $75, North Carolina antique shop, fall 1986.

Apple-Drying Basket

Almost from the very beginning, newcomers to America depended on corn and apples to survive. They had been advised not to drink the water so they drank apple cider. This made apples even more important. When they began to harvest bountiful supplies, they devised other ways of using and preserving them. The winters could be long and hard, so they tried to save as much food as possible for the time they would need it.

One of the things they could do was dry some of the apples. Some peeled the apples to be dried, others didn't, but everybody sliced the apples and put them in a drying basket where they were left until sufficiently dried. The drying baskets could be square or oblong and with or without handles, but they all had an open-weave bottom to allow air to circulate.

Since few people dry apples anymore, the need for apple-drying baskets no longer exists, but they are very collectible. Perhaps they're more collectible for nostalgia than for decorative purposes, the purpose for which they are usually acquired now.

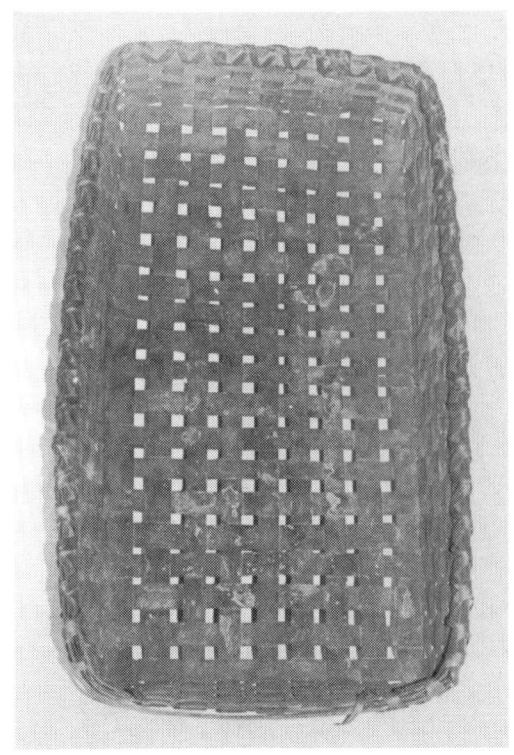

A stain from apples can still be seen in the bottom of this apple-drying basket. 13½" w, 24½" l. $150, New Hampshire mall, fall 1986.

Art Deco basket filled with flowers. 9" w, 17" o.h. $45, Florida antique shop, spring 1986.

Art Deco

Prior to the 1920s, the majority of baskets had been made by hand. Of course, several basket factories had been making plain burden baskets as well as some little fruit and nut baskets for years, but the trend was beginning to change. Now, a few decorative factory-made baskets were coming into the market. Whereas the older baskets had been considered more utilitarian, these new baskets were being introduced for use in the home to hold fruit or freshly cut flowers. Some were so attractive they were used alone; others were used with wicker furniture just as they are today.

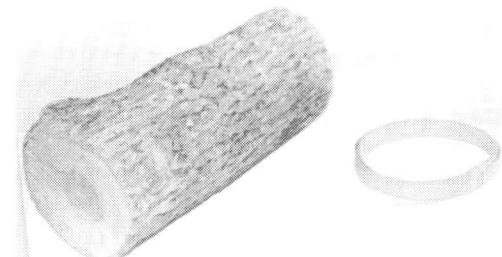

An ash log cut to size with coil of ash splints on the side.

Ash Splints

Without ash splints, the Indians of the Northeast couldn't have made the beautiful baskets for which they are so famous. But there is still some controversy over the type of ash used—the black, the brown, or the white.

Some claim the black and brown are the same. There are other basketmakers who claim there is only one variety of ash—it all depends on where it grows. But the Indians who have used ash for centuries will argue otherwise. They say that only brown ash is perfect for making their kinds of baskets.

Black ash is too brittle to use in basketry, say the Indians, and white is coarse, stiff, and dries out too quickly—but brown is perfect. It's not only tough, it is slow-drying and very flexible. It can also be divided easily into desired widths and thicknesses, which is essential for Northeastern basketmakers, as they only use paper-thin splints in their baskets. It must also be very flexible so that it can be bent and twisted to make all the curly designs.

Ash splints were more widely used than other splint varieties; either that, or more baskets made of ash splints have survived than those made of other splints. Perhaps one of the reasons for the abundance of ash-splint baskets is that these basketmakers continued working long after the oak and hickory basketmakers of the Southern Highlands and the Ozarks had dwindled to only a few.

It was the custom among most tribes for the men to go into the forest where they selected and cut ash trees perfect for basketry. Years of experience taught them the type of tree to look for and the areas where they would most likely be found. One Penobscot Indian man, who has been gathering ash for basketmaking for half a century, says the best ash trees are almost impossible to find now.

Finding the trees and cutting and fetching them home was only part of the chore. Once home, they had to be cut into sections, and then beaten until the annual growth separated. Instead of having to split or rive it like oak, hickory, or elm, ash will separate simply by pounding it with a maul or mallet. It seems that nature and the ash tree are in cooperation with basketmakers as the annual growth, or layers, of ash trees are nearly perfect in size for making the heavier work baskets. For the small fancy baskets with all types of curlicues, the ash tree layers can be divided and subdivided to make paper-thin splints.

Indians were not the only ones to make ash-splint baskets. Soon after the arrival of the white man, he, too, began to make ash-splint baskets for chores around the home and farm. By sharing ideas, they were soon making some of the finest baskets in the world.

Basketmakers like working with ash because it's resistant to decay: You seldom see an ash basket with its bottom rotted away like an oak or hickory basket.

The brown heartwood of the ash was sometimes mixed with the lighter splints from the outside of the tree for a pleasant contrast. Other times, basketmakers would make a few baskets using all-brown heartwood as they didn't like to waste the hard-to-gather splints. This gave the newly made basket the appearance of an old one.

Ash splints may be plaited or woven freehand, or they may be fitted over a mold or form while still green and pliable. Handles on the work, or burden, baskets were generally made of white ash while most of the handles on the fancy baskets were plaited out of sweet grass. Sweet grass and Hong Kong grass were mixed with many of the smaller ash-splint baskets. Viburum and other flexible woods were and still are used in some of the ash-splint baskets, and it is not unusual to find them laced around the top with basswood, or thin roots of spruce or tamarack.

Authentication

Authentication—confirming what an old basket is made of, where it was made, and by whom—is one of the most difficult chores in basketry. By studying and comparing the work of various people in different areas, it does become easier. Another source of assistance can be the many descendants of the old basketmakers who are still making baskets using the methods of their ancestors.

For instance, the Choctaws in Mississippi and the Chitimachas in Louisiana have always used swamp cane or river cane in their basketmaking. The Cherokees also use it, but not as exclusively as the Choctaws and the Chitimachas. The Choctaws and Cherokees use less color (or less vivid colors) than the Chitimachas. The Cherokees also make oak and hickory split baskets as well as a wide variety of vine baskets, as did the early settlers of that area and those of the Ozarks.

With the exception of Chitimacha baskets, both old and new, the old splint baskets made by the North Carolina Cherokees are bringing the best prices today. It's not unusual to find prime examples priced from $500 to $1,500. Their vine baskets, however, are not nearly as popular, nor are they commanding high prices. Prices on their cane baskets range between the splint and vine.

Old Chitimacha baskets are another story, indeed. Owners of old baskets have been offered thousands of dollars for them. The only person known to still be making them is two years behind on orders, and her large baskets are selling for just under $2,000.

Mountain-made baskets have always been popular due to the skill and dedication of the makers. The most popular old ones in this category are the splint baskets that are selling today for prices ranging from $300 to $750. No longer are the poor-quality and damaged ones thrown away; they sell for prices ranging from $25 to $200, depending on quality and condition. Some of the slightly damaged are repaired and put back on the market as good ones.

Not surprisingly, baskets made in a particular area will bring more in that area, which is due, no doubt, to the collector's familiarity with the local types of baskets.

Unless you know the history of an item, the authentication and identification of the actual maker is nearly impossible, since any member of the given community could have made the same type baskets. This problem is not limited to any specific area of the country.

Some basketmakers had basket shops while others would have friends join forces to make baskets during the winter—baskets that would be sold in the spring and summer to help augment low salaries or poor farm prices. This technique of making baskets was prevalent with many groups such as the Shaker and Amana colonies of Iowa, and in areas of the country from New England to the Smoky Mountains.

One Indian chief remembers the group he worked with in the 1930s, making 150 baskets each day. They were making them for their roadside stands and tourist and gift shops.

Baskets made by these different groups are similar, almost identical in some cases, and therefore tricky to authenticate by individual maker. Making it even more difficult is the fact there are no records, and few of the older makers are left.

Dating them is equally as difficult because they were made over such a long period of time. Another problem stems from the new baskets. They can be left outside for six months to a year and will have aged enough to fool the novice. Aging in the South turns them to a golden brown or beige color, almost the same color as the older baskets. In the mountains, aged baskets turn a sort of aged gray, similar to the older ones found there.

The Miccosukees and Seminoles of Florida and the Coushatta Indians of Louisiana have always been famous for their pine needle baskets, although they still make a few swamp-cane baskets.

The Micmac, Penobscot, Passamaquoddy, and Maliseet nations of Maine used predominately ash splint and sweet grass to make their baskets. Other Indian tribes, as well as white basketmakers, used the same materials. This makes it easier to identify the area where the basket was made, but not the maker. The western Indians used yucca, grasses, and rush, along with willow or any other native materials they could find. Indians in the Northwest used plenty of roots and grasses in their baskets.

At one time or another, every basketmaker has used a variety of materials, including the vines growing in their area. Today, kudzu vine is used. And, to confuse basket collectors even more, an avalanche of baskets are arriving daily, it seems, from China and the Philippines. Few, if any, are made like the old bamboo baskets of a century ago, but the workmanship on them is good and prices are cheap. One organization is having *basket parties* on the order of other home-product parties. All of the party baskets we've seen have had tags specifying that they were for that type of sale and that were made in the Philippines. All of the party-type baskets appear to be quite well made; in fact, some of them look like cheap versions of the coiled baskets made by the Western Indians.

Basket prices are high now, and seem to be going higher—for the good, older baskets. In order to avoid costly mistakes in basketry, it's advisable to learn as much as possible about them before venturing into the marketplace. More information and photos of baskets made by each group can be found under specific headings.

Awls like this were necessary to punch holes in the birch bark to make the porcupine quill boxes.

Awls

All basketmakers used an *awl*—a pointed tool for making holes—of one kind or another. Some were made of bone and others from horn, while still another group might prefer to make them from hard oak. Then, there were those made from the thorns of the thorn-apple tree. Recently, a basketmaker was seen using an awl made from the handle of an old spoon. Sailors making Nantucket baskets often used awls made of ivory they found in ports around the world, and from whale's teeth.

Thompson River Indian baby carrier made of the inner bark of cedar, wrapped with grasses. Approximately 25" l. Lightner Museum Collection, NPA.

Baby Carrier

In each Indian tribe, a mother would fashion her baby carrier in the manner that best suited her needs: The baby was fastened in the carrier on its mother's back, allowing her to continue working.

The most beautiful baby carriers were made by the Iroqois and the Thompson River Indians. The workmanship on the old carriers is exquisite. The carrier is a long, beautifully woven basket with buckskin throngs on either end (so the baby could be attached, crosswise, to its mother's back). This was one of the earliest type carriers, and it's possible the babies were later carried in an upright position.

Backpacking Baskets

The Indians were using backpacking baskets when the Pilgrims arrived. They used them to move from one location to another. The very early settlers, especially the trappers, soon adapted the Indian's backpacking baskets to their needs. Backpacking baskets are still made today, and especially used by hikers and campers.

Ash-splint backpacking basket, probably made by the Penobscot Indians. 9" by 15" w, 18" h. $75, New England antique mall, fall 1986.

Each tribe designed its backpack to suit the tribe's needs. The Micmacs and Penobscots made the finest ones. They're all approximately the same size and in the shape of a medium-sized wastebasket. Others, though, are fancier, with more ornate designs on the corners and around the tops.

The above photo shows a backpack with heavy straps.

Balloon Basket

For the most part, only museums are interested in old balloon baskets, but as the hobby of ballooning continues to grow, so will the demand for new baskets, and there is a chance the older ones will become more popular. They're still being made both here and in England.

Originally, balloon baskets were made of willow, but in recent years, makers in the United States have imported rattan from the Philippines. In England, basketmakers still use the more plentiful willow.

Civil War balloon basket. Army Aviation Museum, Ft. Rucker, Alabama, NPA.

Old brown bamboo basket painted blue. 7¼" dia, 13" h. $15, Maine mall, winter 1987.

It is likely that woven baskets will continue to be used with balloons as they are lighter than most other material that could be used. Woven baskets are also safe and flexible in case the balloon loses power and lands on or near power lines.

Balm of Gilead

Balm of Gilead is a small evergreen tree of the myrrh family. It's a native of Asia and Africa. In America, the cultivated variety is called American Balsam fir and is grown from Maine to Minnesota. The roots were used to weave baskets that needed heavy bases.

Bamboo

American bamboo is of little use to basketmakers. Most bamboo baskets are made in the Orient from bamboo grown there, the kind that florishes in the East. It is a treelike tropical plant growing to heights of

Later bamboo drying basket. 21" w, 8" h. $25, Vermont mall, winter 1987.

one hundred feet. (Actually, it is more like a reed than a tree, but grows so large and tall it becomes tree-like.)

Mature Oriental bamboo stalks can be as wide as six feet in diameter and strong enough to be used in house-building, making furniture, and for ship masts. The medium-sized stalks are used for canes and basketry, while the young shoots are used for food.

In years past, both the Chinese and Japanese were noted for the rich brown color of their best bamboo baskets. The color was not achieved with dyes, but by searching out old pieces of bamboo from houses being torn down and destroyed. It mellows to just the right shade from years of use and smoke.

Basket Forms or Molds

Wooden forms over which baskets were woven. See Form for Baskets.

Basket Handles

Handles for baskets range from ordinary to elegant, if basket handles can be classified as elegant. Most over-the-top handles are of plain, but tough, oak, ash, or hickory splints. The handle may have a design carved or whittled on it, or it could be lashed onto the basket quite elegantly. It's interesting to find two almost identical baskets with the handles on the sides of one and on the ends of the other. But the ingenuity of our ancestors is never more visible than in the carving and attaching of handles on burden bushel baskets. It was imperative that the handles hold, especially if one was carrying precious seeds or foods; therefore, they not only carved them to fit so their weight would rest on a sturdy point, they also wove the handle into the basket for reinforcement.

Circa 1920 baby scales. 13" w, 20" l. $45, Florida antique shop, spring 1986.

Basket for Baby Scales

In the 1920s and later, it was the custom to weigh one's baby at home. For this chore, one needed baby scales with a basket so the tiny infant could rest comfortably while being weighed. Manufacturers, always anxious to please the buying public, introduced a variety of baby scales, all with woven, beribboned baskets.

Today, baby-scale baskets aren't used much, but they're part of the basketry/wicker scene and should be saved if only to complete one's basketry collection.

Reinforced handle on bushel basket.

Basketmaker

Basketmaker is a word commonly used to describe anyone who makes baskets, but in the old Indian culture it was used to describe the transitional life of the early Indians of the Southwest. In the beginning, they lived very primitively. The Indians were simply small-game hunters who used primitive spears, snares, and nets. For their other food, they depended on whatever was growing wild in the area, but even for that time (between 1 and 400 A.D.) they are credited with making beautiful baskets. Many of those old baskets have been found and dated by teams who established digs in the area in 1880. One of the most surprising things about the digs was the number of finer baskets found turned upside down over the faces of the deceased. It's believed archaeologists were the first to use the term *Basketmaker* for the people of that period, and they coined it because of the many exquisite baskets they found in the digs.

Researchers continued to use the word to describe the next period (400 to 700 A.D.) when the Indians of the Southwest moved from Desert Culture to Agriculture. Not a booming agriculture, to be sure, but a beginning. At least they began growing some corn and squash, maybe other foods. This period is referred to as *Basketmaker II*.

Their lifestyles continued to improve during *anasazi* or the third period (700 to 1100 A.D.); they began to build houses of wattle and daub, wear cotton clothing, and they continued to make baskets of all kinds. Sometime during this period they began observing rich ceremonials that necessitated the use of fine handicrafts, especially elegant items of basketry. There was one exception—the Tarahumaras who developed a lifestyle much like the first Basketmakers. They continued living that style for centuries.

Basket with handles on the ends.

Identical basket with handles on either side.

The handle goes around the basket for strength and reinforcement.

Old picture of a basketmaker taking her wares to town.

Basketmaker's Pack Basket

Some basketmakers, especially those who only depended on selling baskets to supplement other income, usually took their baskets to town on horseback, in a buggy or wagon, or on their own backs. For the latter chore, they usually made large baskets similar to the backpacking peat baskets or the later clothes hampers. The baskets had to be as light as possible as they would be piled high with smaller baskets.

Basswood

Basswood is used in basketmaking today much as it was a century ago. It can be boiled if toughness is required, but in most cases, the inner bark—after it has been cut into long, thin strips and placed among rushes on the edge of a lake—can be used just as it is, peeled and separated from the outer bark. When necessary, it can be twisted into twine that can be used to weave either mats for the floor or can be used to fasten coiled baskets. Like most of the materials used by the old basketmakers, basswood strips could be gathered, separated, and wrapped into coils to be used when needed.

Beaded Basket

The sight of this basket conjures up visions of the South Sea Islands. But closer inspection shows that a tremendous amount of work was required to sew on all the tiny beads. It also has a round tin insert in the top—very unusual, but probably made to be carried on one's head.

Origin, material, and use are unknown, but the workmanship is superb. Thousands of tiny beads have been hand-sewn on the bottom and over fabric sewn on first in special places.

Beaded basket. 10" dia, 3½" h, $55, New England flea market, fall 1986.

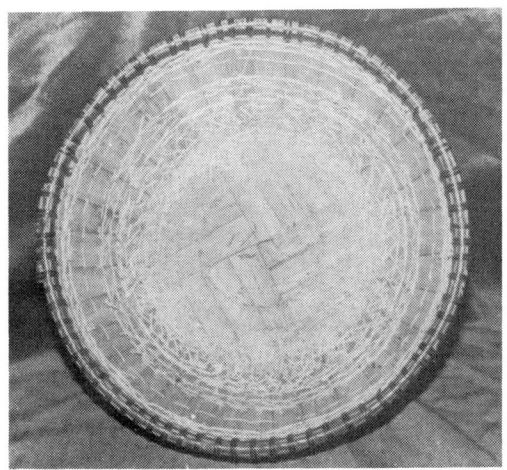

Inside of basket showing how beads were sewn on.

Rye beehive. Blount Mansion, NPA.

Beehives

Long before the introduction of wooden beehives, beekeepers made hives of coiled rye. Those who preferred the rye or straw hives used them for years, probably from habit, but it is known that they continued to use them for years after others were using wooden hives. In fact, some continued to use them until they were outlawed—it was thought they might harbor diseases harmful to the bees.

Basket beehives were inexpensive, as everyone had rye straw, and they were easy to make. The maker only had to coil enough rye straw to make a hive of the size he wanted. Then, he made a small opening in the front for the bees to leave and return, and as soon as he installed a frame in the bottom to hold the honey, he was in business. This style beehive is believed to have originated with the Pennsylvania Dutch, who called them *skeps*. Old rye beehives are not too plentiful, but new ones, some quite crude, are being made.

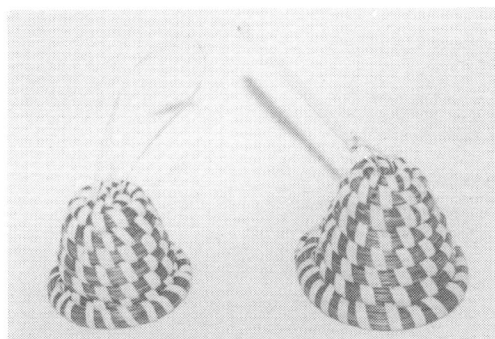

Two Gullah-made bells. Large size, 2½" dia, 2" h; small 2" dia, 1½" h; $3 and $4, Gullah roadside stand, spring 1986.

Bells

It is little wonder that the history of bells has been lost in the sea of antiquity when we realize they've been used in China for over 46 centuries. During that time, they've been made of nearly every known material, and used in as many different ways.

So it shouldn't be surprising to find that they were, and still are, being made in basketry. The Gullahs of South Carolina are making small hanging bells of sea grass and palmetto. They have also been made of rattan. Both are late, and the latter is used at weddings, and to hold mistletoe at Christmas.

Rattan bell. 6" dia, 6" h. Under $5 wherever found.

Swamp-cane double-woven belt. Private collection, NPA.

Belt

Skilled basketmakers have to test themselves occasionally by making something not heretofore made. This was the case of the Stouff family years ago when they not only designed, but made, a double-woven belt. It is made of finely cut strips of swamp cane dyed in bright colors—colors that have faded some through the years. Double weaving requires expertise many basketmakers don't have, and to make a belt requires ingenuity, skill, and patience.

Crudely made bark-berry picking basket. 6" square, 12" o.h. $18, Florida antique shop, spring 1986.

Berry Basket

Since the settlers and the Indians depended so much on berries of all kinds, it was only natural that they made special berry-picking baskets. Some were made of wooden splints while others were made of different barks. They were not made to be works of art, but rather primitive baskets they could take to the woods and fields without fear of ruining them with berry stains.

Birch-bark basket with scalloped top. 6" h, 7" dia. $3, Maine barn sale, fall 1986.

Birch Bark

The bark of the birch tree was used for many things. The white settlers soon learned from the Indians that it could be used to make everything from canoes to baskets. Birch bark was used to make dishes, funnels,cooking utensils, fans, covering for dwellings, and makuks (a primitive but useful container that might be used for storing food, maple syrup, or water—if the seams were waterproof).

The reason for birch bark's popularity and usefulness was its abundance and its variety of thicknesses. For instance, the heaviest bark from large trees might have six to nine distinct layers and be strong enough to make a large canoe. On other trees, the bark was almost paper thin, but still strong enough to hold light items like food.

Birch-bark baskets and other items made from the bark often split with age. But the splits were easily mended using the gum from the balsam. This feature was very attractive to the women whose baskets might split while they were out gathering berries—she could mend quickly and resume her berry gathering.

Crooked knife or bikahlagenigan *with a basket.*

Bikahlagenigan

This is the Penobscot name for the crooked knife used by most basketmakers. It's one of the essential tools in basketry. They call the regular knife sekwak while the plural is sekwagol. There is little demand for the knives today as most basketmakers have their own. It is most often used to help collectors understand how the old baskets were made.

25

Birch-bark basket applied design, new. $65, gift shop, fall 1986.

Covered birch-bark etched design basket. 4½" w, 3½" h. $25, gift shop, fall 1986.

Side of porcupine quill decorated birch-bark box, 2½" h, 3½" w. Unity College collection, NPA.

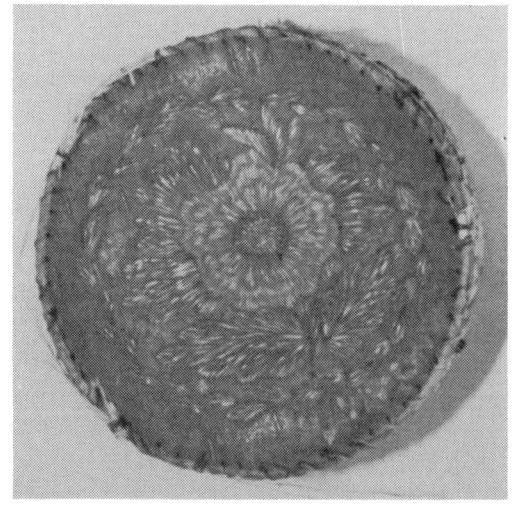

Birch-bark box with moose-hair embroidery. Unity College collection, NPA.

Birch-bark baskets range from the crude, vine-handled berry baskets to the more sophisticated examples with beautiful etched designs on the sides. Some were made of lighter bark and trimmed with darker bark.

Birch bark was, and still is, used as the foundation for porcupine quill boxes and baskets. The quills are fastened to the top layer of birch, then lined with another layer so the quills will be covered. All this is fastened together with spruce roots or basswood. Moose-hair embroidery was also done on birch bark as well as on leather.

Collection of Baskets

Picnic Baskets

(l to r) Small Splint, Bushwhacker, Half-Bushel, and Freehand-Designed Baskets

Block- or Potato-Printed Bonnet Basket

Three Small Nantucket Baskets

Plain Ash-Splint Storage Basket

Ash-Splint Storage Basket

Assortment of Baskets

(l to r) Peach Basket, Storage Basket, and Feather Basket

Collection of Small Basketry Items

Moose-Hair Embroidered Birch-Bark Box

Porcupine Quill Boxes and Beaded Baskets

From the Unity College Collection of Baskets

From the Unity College Collection of Baskets

From the Unity College Collection of Baskets

From the Unity College Collection of Baskets

Old picture of a basketry bird nest.

Basket with block printing. 15" h, 20" dia. $175, Vermont mall, fall 1986.

Bird Nest

Bird nests were one of the easiest basketry items to make, and today they are very available. Perhaps large numbers were made and left in the trees to deteriorate.

Apparently, the idea originated at the Bird Market in Paris where they were sold in large numbers around the turn of the century. An important rule in making bird nests was to make them as inconspicuous as possible—birds like nests that are natural looking. Suggested materials for making them were willow, twigs, and grasses, or they could be made of the same materials—twig spokes and rush weavers—as those sold at the Paris Bird Market.

Bishop, Ralph

Contemporary Maine basketmaker, and the only white man known to still be making porcupine quill baskets.

Block Printing

Originally, designs were painted on baskets in a freehand or geometric design. Later, for those unable to make the simple designs, or for those preferring an easier method, block printing (also called potato printing) was devised. Indications are that this type decoration originated with the Algonkian tribes.

For block or potato printing, a basketmaker would cut a design on a potato or block of wood. Next, the design would be dipped into a plant stain or other dyes before applying it to the spokes or weavers.

Blood-Root

The inner bark of the roots of this plant was used to make a red or orange dye, depending on how it was used. A century ago, Indians used a handful of blood-root, mixed with a handful of wild plums in a quart of hot water, to make a deep red that was said to make an exellent dye for porcupine quills—quills that would later be used to decorate boxes and baskets. Fresh blood-root rubbed on wooden splints produces an orangey shade.

Blue Dye

See Indigo.

Blueberries

Blueberries were used to make a reddish-pink dye for use in basketry. Also see Red Dye.

Bone

The awl-like instrument used by the Gullah basket makers of South Carolina. The first ones were made of bone, hence the name, but more recently they are making them from old spoon handles.

Bonnet Basket

Some believe these popular baskets originated in New Hampshire, but it's a well-known fact that they were made all over New England. Many feel these baskets were made by settlers and Indians, but most were probably made by the Indians who sold them to the settlers.

Some were square based with round covers, indicating they had some difficulty converting the basket's original square form to a round shape. But that skill was mastered and bonnet baskets were eventually made in all shapes.

For home use they were large enough to hold quite a bit of clothing or several bonnets at one time. This was a time when storage containers and storage space was at a premium. They were low enough to be stored under the high beds, and they were also a popular substitute for the hat or bandbox when traveling by stagecoach or packet.

Earlier examples have been seen covered with chintz, round at the bottom and with a drawstring at the top. The cover served a dual role—it kept dust out of the clothing and bonnets stored therein, and it kept the basket clean and new looking. In fact, one will be seen from time to time that looks almost new, and chances are it was kept covered, or maybe put in the attic long after it was no longer used.

Ash-splint bonnet basket with block printing. 15" h, 20" dia. $175, Vermont mall, fall 1986.

Penobscot-made bonnet basket of ash splints.

Most of the bonnet baskets were made of rather wide ash splints, not cut too thin so they would be sturdy and serviceable. Many have potato or block printing. Bonnet baskets seem to have originated around the late 1700s and their popularity continued until around 1860—later in some areas.

Late Indian-made ash and sweet-grass bonnet basket. Unity College collection, NPA.

Orange and yellow ash-splint and sweet-grass bookmarks. 8" and 10" h, 2½" dia. $5 each, Maine mall, 1987.

Bookmarks

During the early part of this century (about 1913 to 1929), a period in basketry that could rightfully be called the Souvenir Age, both Indians and whites in the Northeast made any and everything they thought the visiting tourist would buy. Some of the easiest and inexpensive items to make were the ash-splint and sweet-grass bookmarks. They were easily made from the leftovers of other projects. At five cents each, bookmarks were priced so a family could afford a dozen or more.

Boston Ivy

In basketry the larger vines can be used as spokes while the smaller ones are split to make fine weavers. Examples are hard to find, and even harder to authenticate unless, of course, one is a botanist.

Bottle or Jug, Basketry Covered

Basketry-covered bottles and jugs made in the 1800s could be any size from a pint to a gallon, but most were in the quart to half-gallon sizes. The basketry covers might be made of willow or oak splints, depending on what the company wanted.

Reports indicate that both whites and Indians were employed to make the covers. In the Northeast, they were often made of ash splints. The basketry covers were used to protect the glass bottle, often brown ones, from breakage in shipping. Handles were added to make it easier to take the bottle or jug back for a refill. The making of basketry-covered bottles and jugs ceased nearly a century ago in the states, but various types of alcoholic beverages were bottled in basketry-covered containers until the 1970s. Most of the more recent covers were made in Italy.

Brown half-gallon jug in basketry. $25, Maine antique show, fall 1986.

Bottoms Up

The bottom of a basket is often a clue to the skills of the maker and the sturdiness and lasting quality of the basket. Some baskets have a reinforced bottom with exposed spokes. Others, like one of the large storage baskets, have a rim woven halfway between the center and the outside, while still another will have a wide splint around the outside of the bottom. Then there are baskets with extra weavers or spokes added to each corner, and they extend down to form short legs. On a loosely woven bottom, this would allow air to circulate more freely. Baskets were made with runner-type splints on the bottom. They not only protected the bottom, but could be used to slide it along without damaging the splint bottom.

Passamaquoddy-made basketry cover of sweet grass and ash splints. 9" h, 2" dia bottom, ¾" dia top. $35, Maine antique show, fall 1986.

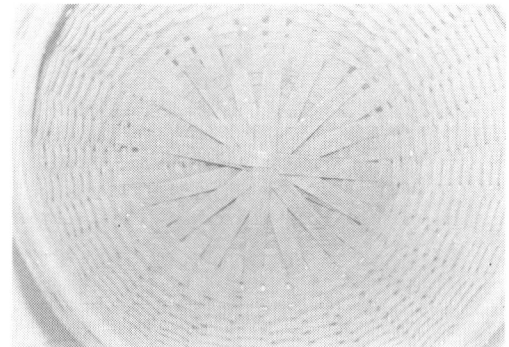

Reinforced bottom.

Raised woven ring on bottom of basket.

Basket with runner-type splints on the bottom.

Extra spokes were added on each corner to form legs.

Heavy rim on bottom of round basket.

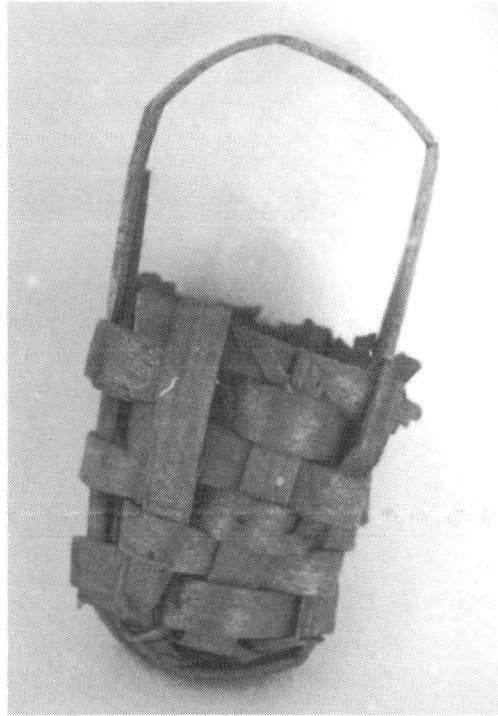
Tiny bracelet basket. ¾" dia, 1½" o.h. $5 as novelty, Maine antique show, 1987.

Bracelet Baskets

Whether or not these tiny baskets were ever worn on bracelets is unknown. If they were, it was probably to advertise the maker's wares. They were used occasionally to decorate other pieces of basketry. The Penobscots, Malisetts, and Pasamaquoddies were among the most prolific makers of bracelet baskets while the Micmacs only made a few. Other basketmakers may have made them as well.

Braided handle.

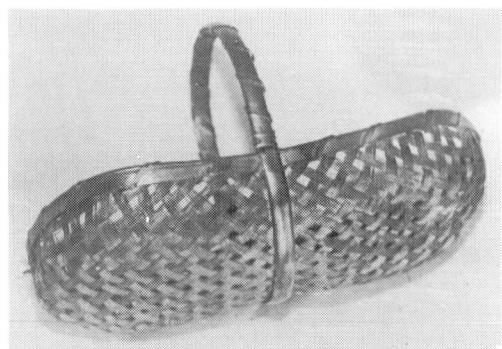

Brass basket. 5½" l, 3" o.h. $5, Maine antique show, fall 1986.

Braided Handles

Braided handles were used more on vine and cane baskets, although there are cases where they were used on other types of baskets. The braids could be made of 3, 9, or 12 strands, and were braided like hair. Finely cut splints could be used as could cane, reed, rattan, sweet, and Hong Kong grass.

Braiding

See Plaiting.

Braken

Any number of large, coarse ferns whose roots were gathered, cleaned, and split to be used in basketry. It was especially useful in making dark patterns.

Brass Baskets

Many different materials have been used to make baskets. Some have worked well; others not so well. The materials that worked were used repeatedly while the others were not. Brass is a metal, and apparently didn't work well in basketry. Brass has, though, been used to make some small, decorative baskets.

Bread-Raising Baskets

The German immigrants who settled in Pennsylvania are believed to be the first to make dough- or bread-raising baskets. Whether or not they were the first doesn't matter when you consider the large number they made. These baskets are usually called *Mennonite* baskets and were usually made of rye.

Other basketmakers, using whatever materials were available, produced some of coiled-wrapped straw. In the early days, these baskets were used exclusively for bread raising. After the introduction of tin and graniteware bread raisers, these baskets might have been used for any household chore.

Bread-raising basket. 14" dia, 5½" h. $35, Rhode Island antique show, fall 1986.

Brome Grass

In checking the various grasses used in basketmaking, we found there were at least a half dozen species of each with different ones growing in different areas. This meant the basketmaker used the variety that was most convenient. But then basketmakers were never too concerned with species or botanical names; they called all the materials by the common names used in their area. In this case, *brome* was derived from the Greek *bormos,* a kind of oat. None of the species of brome grass were eaten by cattle or horses because it was too tough. But the split stems were used to an advantage in basketry—to make a white design in split-root baskets.

Brown Dye

Brown dye could be made from several things, but walnut bark was the favorite for making dark brown dye. The bark could also be used for making black dye by using additional ingredients and a longer boiling time. A light, soft brown dye was made from the bark of butternut.

Brown Jar, Basketry Covered

Several things came in brown jars during the first decades of this century, but the item most often found was snuff. Many women saved and found alternative uses for these jars rather than discard them.

Brown jar covered with ash splints and Hong Kong grass. 3¼" dia, 6" h, $17. Maine auction, fall 1986.

They were often used for canned fruits and vegetables. Today the jars are collected as advertising items since they have the information about the snuff companies on the sides and the lids. Apparently, covering a brown jar with basketry was not only a way to save it, but a challenge.

Buck Basket

Buck basket is the term used in some parts of the country to describe the laundry basket. It originated from the word *buck* which described lye or soapsuds used to wash clothes.

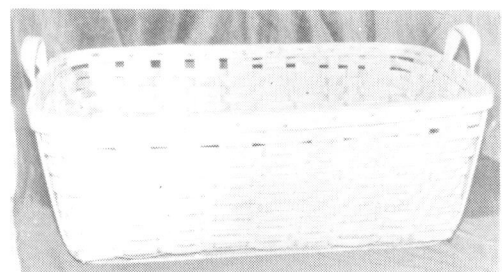

Factory-made oak-splint buck or laundry basket. 19" w, 29" l. $10, Maine flea market, fall 1986.

Handmade oak-splint buck or laundry basket. 23" w, 27" l. $75, Missouri auction, summer 1986.

Bushwhacker basket. 18" dia, 13" h. $135, Maine auction, fall 1986.

Bushwacker Baskets

It's physically impossible to identify every old basket with its maker. But as more and more research is done, the history of many baskets is surfacing.

For years, numerous sturdy baskets could be found, but they defied authentication. They were usually referred to as *Shaker* or Shaker-type. Then, two basket researchers found they had been made by some very skilled basketmakers in the village of Taghkanic, New York. The researchers, Martha Wetherbee and Nathan Taylor, found the people had been living in the mountains for centuries making and selling their baskets. They became known as *bushwhackers,* a name that was to imply they didn't know how to do anything other than live in the hills, marry each other, and make baskets.

They are also known as *Taconic* baskets because the name of the village has since been simplified to Taconic. But whatever the name, they have made some of the finest authenticated baskets in the country. Once the genuine baskets have been studied, they are more easily recognized. All of the baskets are made of ash and oak splints, and the most desirable ones have round tops and bottoms, and swing handles.

Bushwhacker baskets were made by the thousands during the years they were made so prolifically. Like so many other basketmakers, these people made baskets all winter to be sold in the spring and summer, and like the others, they suffered a loss of income when the paper bag replaced the basket.

Butterweed

A wild flower with a yellow daisy-like blossom that was used to make yellow dye. Grown abundantly in Louisiana, maybe in other areas as well. Also called *yellow top.*

Oak-splint buttocks basket. 11" dia, 13" h. $250, Kentucky antique mall, spring 1986.

Buttocks Baskets

Buttock basket is another name for the gizzard basket, one of the market-type baskets. The center rib or spoke is indented so that it resembles both a gizzard and a buttock.

The shape of this basket allowed it to be easily and comfortably carried on the hip. Presumably this was done to distribute the weight and make it easier to carry the burden.

New Cajun-made oak-splint basket. 17" dia, 8" h, $26, Louisiana gift shop. spring 1986.

Cajun Baskets

The Cajuns of Louisiana were excellent basketmakers, but there is little demand for their baskets today. A few makers still weave the old oak-splint baskets, but the paper bag and box have all but eliminated the need for baskets. In earlier years they made rice baskets, but now the rice is harvested with machines.

Rattan cake basket. 10" dia, 9" h. $22, South Carolina antique shop, spring 1986.

Cake Baskets

Years ago, there were very few bakeries. Housewives were proud of their culinary skills, and couldn't resist the temptation to take a freshly baked cake to every social event, and for the baked goods to arrive in perfect condition, they needed special cake carriers. (Even at home they could use the perfect serving dish.) Manufacturers heard the cry, and answered with cake baskets in silver, porcelain, and glass. Basketmakers also became aware of the trend and made less expensive models in every material from oak splints to coiled pine needles.

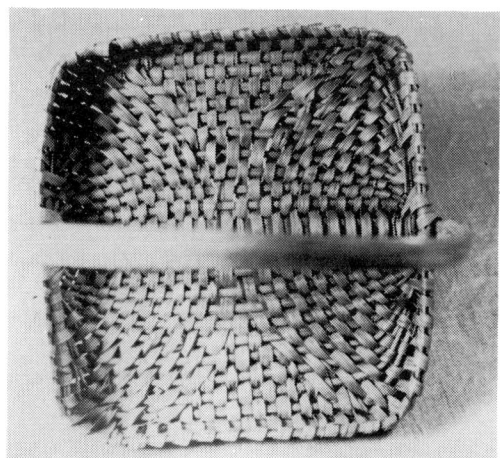

Square oak-splint cake basket. Private collection, NPA.

Round oak-splint cake basket. Private collection, NPA.

The home and its furnishings were of utmost importance to the Victorian ladies, as each was judged by her peers on the condition and appearance of her home—and the way she entertained. In the mountain areas of Tennessee (west and north), homemakers seemed to opt for oak-splint cake baskets, but in the Northeast, it was ash and sweet grass.

White rattan candy basket. 10" dia, 3" h. $5, Maine auction, summer 1986.

Candy Basket

Dozens of variations of this rattan basket were made from instructions given in the basketry books published nearly a century ago, and they were all called *candy baskets*. These are the same baskets you see so often holding yarn in the "country home" pictures. Loosely woven versions of the candy basket are the most available. They vary in size from 7 to 13 inches in diameter, and 2 to 5 inches in height. Prices vary from $2 at a barn or garage sale to as much as $15 at antique shows. Some are natural and others are stained a dark brown, but most have been painted white.

Before women went into the work place, they entertained frequently at home. It might be a large family dinner, or it could be afternoon tea. Afternoon tea was the custom in England, and when they came to America, many of the English brought the custom with them.

Cane, Swamp, or River

A number of plants, similar to bamboo, that have long, willowy reed-like stalks are called *cane*. The word *cane* is used frequently by basket collectors, but among basketmakers, it's identified by the area where it is grown.

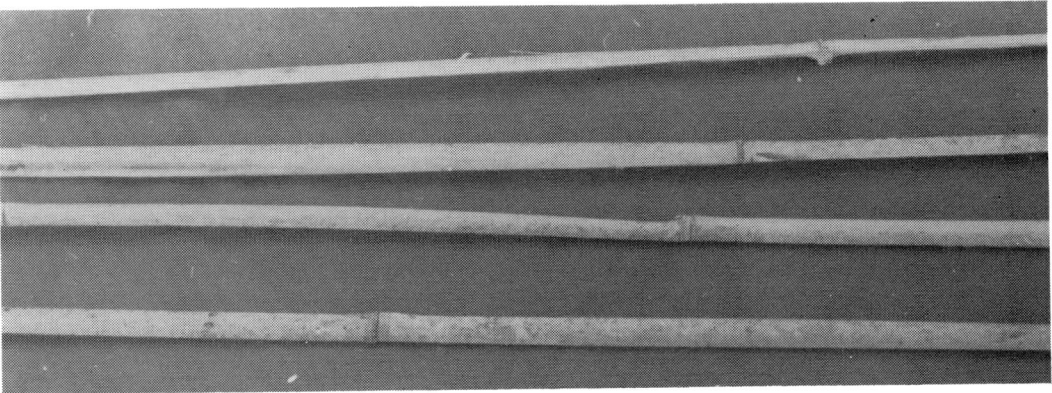
Cane from the first split.

The Cherokees and mountain basketmakers call it *river cane,* while the Mississippi and Louisiana Indians call it *swamp cane.* In the mountain areas it is generally found along the river banks. Further south it is called swamp cane. One Choctaw basketmaker said she had to travel as far as two miles into the swamps to find good cane. What she finally found and cut had to be carried out the same way she came in—on foot.

In Louisiana, the Chitimachas go along the bayous to find the best canebrakes (thickets). In the best canebrakes, cane grows close together, the air is hot and sticky, and the area is filled with mosquitos. And, wherever there is cane, there is danger of snakes—no better place does the canebrake rattler thrive than in the bayous. But cane basketmakers will go where necessary to get the best cane—long, straight stalks with long joints—for their baskets.

Gathering and preparing any basket materials can be a long, drawn-out process, but cane is the most time-consuming of all. It has to be gathered—and in the case of the Choctaws, carried a couple of miles through the swamps—then it must be kept damp until it can be split. The first split is made by notching one end of the round stalk with a sharp knife. The strips are split and split again until they are all less than a half-inch wide each. Actually, they are each only a bit wider than one-fourth inch. The outside layer is held in the teeth and peeled with the hands to remove the pithy center. For the next two weeks, the strips are left outside for dew to fall on them. During that time, the cane strips will lose their natural green color and turn a soft golden brown.

For those who want even finer strips, the cane strips may be split once again. Either way, once they've reached the golden brown color, they are ready to be dyed or used as is.

Canteen

The origin of these woven grass-covered canteens is unknown. An antique dealer bought them at an estate auction in New England but was unable to get any historical information about them. Their tops are stoppers rather than screw-on lids, and their shape is similar to some of the old wine bottles, but there is no explanation for the long shoulder straps unless they were to be taken on hiking trips. The covers are not woven on the bottles as are other kinds; instead, they are attached in three pieces—one on either side and another on the bottom. The seams are covered with a heavy twill-type material and resemble braids; they are hand sewn. The straps or cords are fastened with handstitching near the top.

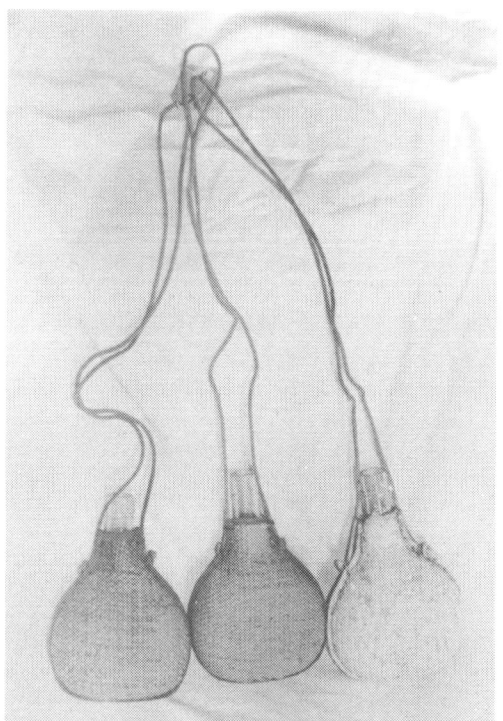

Three canteens with woven grass covers. Bottle is 8" h, 5½" w. $5 each, Maine flea market, summer 1986.

Cat Basket

Another late bloomer in the basketry field, cat baskets, were made in two styles: the covered basket shown in the photograph and the open basket type that resembles a small, oblong laundry basket. These baskets probably date around the same period as the cat carrier, and were still being made a few years ago. So many new basketry items are made in China and the Philippines, it is possible they are still being made. Traditionally, a pillow was placed in the bottom of the basket, and the basket was usually kept in the den, or other room in which the family spent most of its leisure time. Some cat baskets have been painted white and now hold fuzzy toy kittens.

Willow cat carrier with lightweight iron door. $65, Florida antique shop, spring 1986.

Cat Carrier

Cat carriers are also late bloomers. It's very possible some of the early basketmakers had cats they treasured and made carriers for them, but the photograph shown here

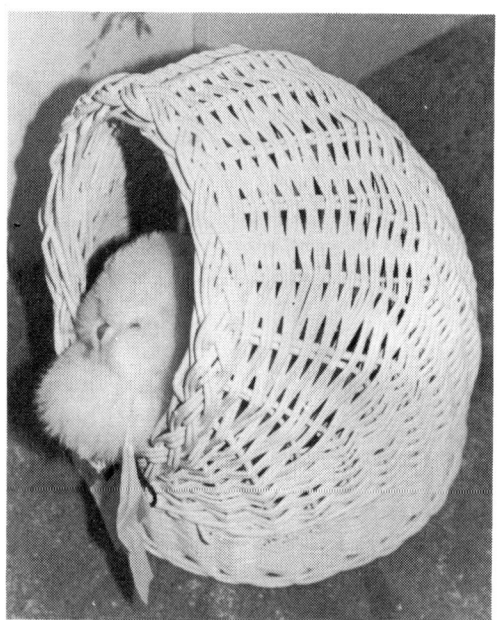

White cat basket. 16" h, 16" w. $35, Florida antique shop, spring 1986.

is one of the oldest we've seen. Prior to the last half century, cats were not usually house pets, but rather lived around the barn and outside buildings. It is only recently that owners began taking their cats on trips that would require a cat carrier.

Cattails

A cattail is a tall reed-like marsh plant with long leaves and a brown, fuzzy, cylindrical flower. The stalks are used in basketry. Gatherers who aren't too familiar with different plants often confuse rush, flag, and cattails, but all will work well in basketry. All three are found in moist places from marshes and lowlands to the banks of sluggish streams.

Some species of cattail grow as high as eight to ten feet tall, while the majority only attain heights of four to five feet. The taller cattails are more desirable for basketmaking. The color and texture of cattails will vary from one stream to another and from one part of the country to another, indicating that their different appearances are dependent, somewhat, on the type of soil found in the marshes.

Cattail, like cane, can be split and dyed for basketmaking, and when mixed with cane, can be mistaken for cane.

Cedar

Both the roots and bark of cedar have been used in basketry. Cedar roots have been used for years, and some baskets made from them are watertight, provided the weaving and twining is tight enough. Split fiberous cedar roots were used for many types of basketry—the Wampalnoags used them to a great advantage, making eel traps. They would split the long cedar roots and wrap them with smaller ones.

The bark of red cedar was also used in basketry—to make pack or flat baskets.

Mention cedar and the average person thinks of a cedar chest, or a closet lined with cedar—it is supposed to inhibit moths and other insects that attack clothing. However, cedar reached an earlier popularity as basket material.

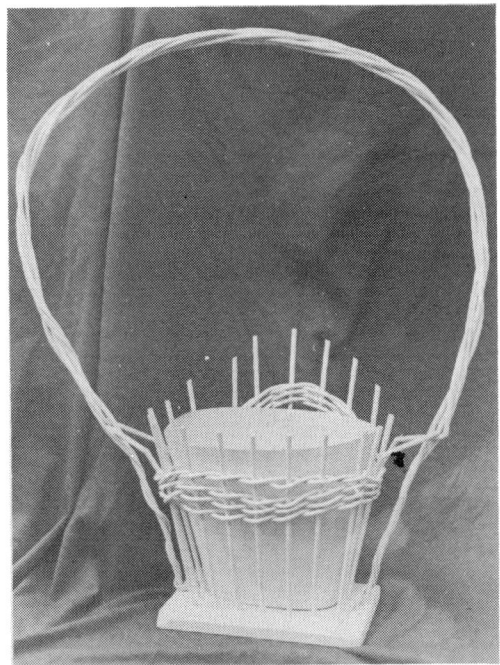

White cemetery flower basket. 15" dia, 35" o.b. $3, yard sale, 1986.

Cemetery Flower Baskets

Half a century or so ago, cemetery arrangements were made from fresh flowers usually cut from one's own garden. These were arranged in poorly woven, inexpensive baskets with metal containers. Florists used the same type baskets. Some families would leave the baskets on graves and put fresh flowers in them from time to time. A few families would even use these baskets at home to hold fresh flowers. When a newer or better container was found, the old ones were discarded or relegated to the attic.

This type basket was used both in the home and at funerals. 14" dia, 29" o.h. $7.50, Maine antique shop, 1986.

Chatelaine

Chatelaine is French for "lady of the castle," or "mistress of the chateau." It is also the word for a long waist chain with a pendant clasp, that ladies wore years ago to hold their purses, keys, and other valuables.

With the passing of time, customs changed, and by the time Victorian ladies began designing chatelaines, they dispensed with the long waist chain. Long waist chains were replaced with a simpler chatelaine, one that fastened on the waistband of a skirt or dress. The later chatelaines were not only different in style, they were generally made of sterling silver, although a few plated ones were made. Several silver chains were fastened to the waistband plate, and each of these chains had a swivel end from which hung scissors, keys, needlecases, a pencil, and maybe a penknife and scent bottle.

When the Indians and whites of the Northeast began making basketry items for tourists, they copied old ideas they thought would sell. One of those was the

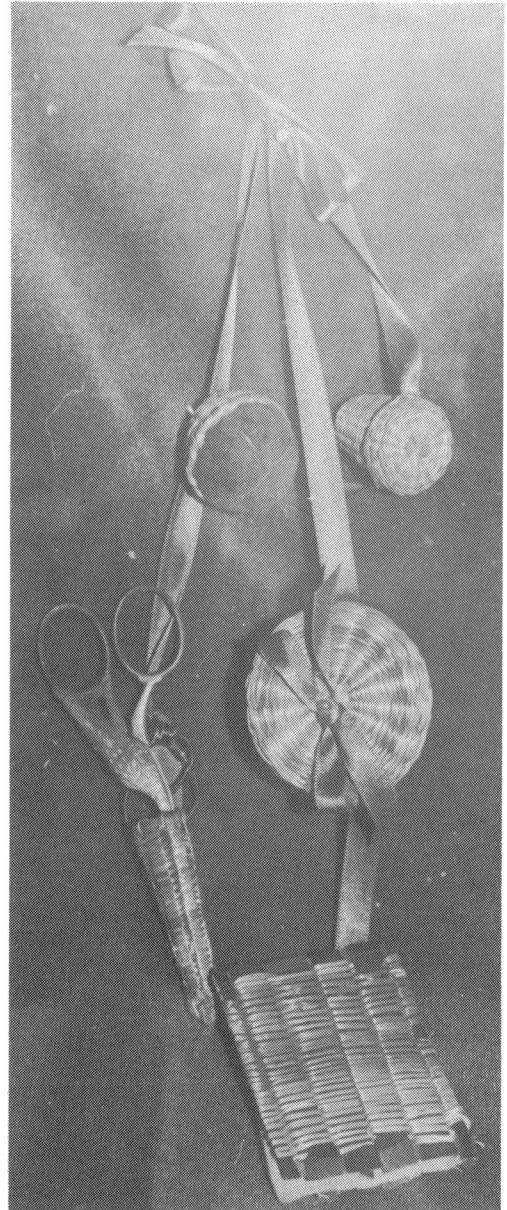

Sweet-grass and ash-splint chatelaine with sterling thimble and scissors. $150, Maine antique shop, winter 1987.

chatelaine which they made of sweet grass and finely cut ash splints. Their version, held together with ribbon, included a booklet filled with flannel, for needles; a small basket for spools of thread; a woven velvet-covered sweet-grass pin cushion; a thimble holder; and a small case for scissors.

Woven disc with metal thimble and no scissors. $38, Maine auction, Fall 1986.

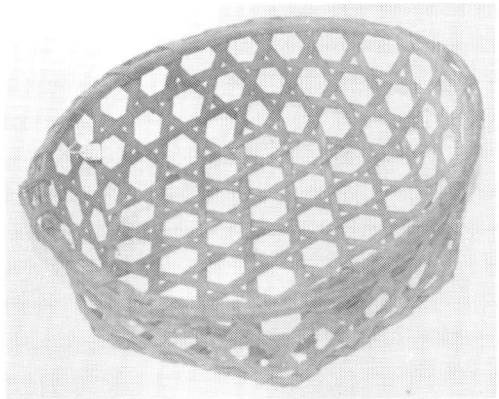

Hexagon-shaped cheese basket. 22" dia, 5" h. $375, New Hampshire mall, fall 1986.

These more contemporary sweet-grass and ash-splint chatelaines probably were not used in the same manner as the original chatelaine. Chatelaines were used by housewives who would hang them on their walls in order to easily find their sewing tools.

The Penobscot and Passamaquoddy Indians were the most prolific makers of chatelaines, and either they, or others, made a variation—a disc with the thread basket, thimble, and scissors holder.

Cheese Basket

Less than a century ago, nearly every family in the country owned a cow. They used the excess milk to make butter and cheese. Making the butter wasn't such a big chore, but making cheese was a long, drawn out process. First, the milk had to be left in a warm place until it soured and formed curds. The cheese basket (usually a hexagon-weave basket) was lined with cloth, filled with the curds, and placed on a rack over a vat that would catch the dripping whey. Later, the curds were put into a cheese mold, and in due time, the family had homemade cheese.

Round cheese mold. 20" dia, 4" h. $350, Maine auction, summer 1986.

Cheese Mold

Every effort was made to find out why an antique dealer in a New Hampshire mall labeled this basket "cheese mold." We was unable to find the owner and the mall manager didn't know. Others who might have known were queried, but no one could vouch for its authenticity. Several thought it could be a small mold, just large enough for one family. The hole in the bottom could have been made to allow the excess whey to continue to drip. So far, the material has defied identification.

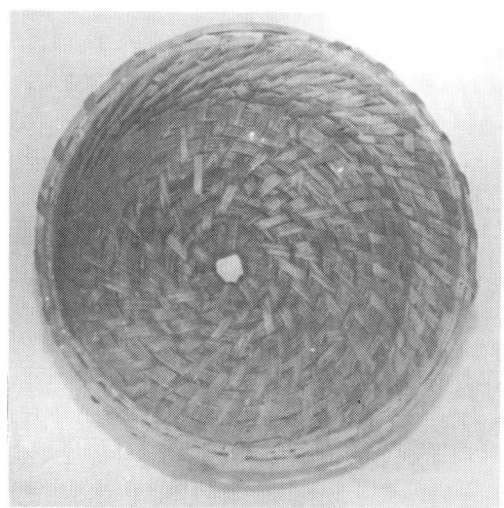

Basketry cheese mold. 8½" dia, 3½" h. $35, New Hampshire mall, fall 1986.

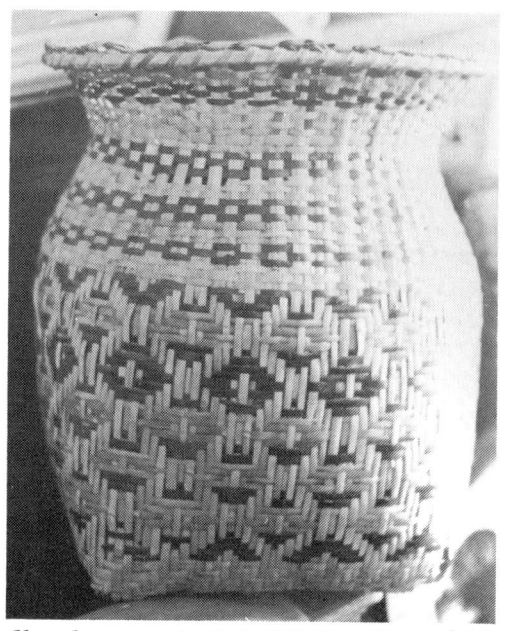

Cherokee cane basket. 16" dia, 19" h. $750, Tennessee auction, fall 1985.

Cherokee cane basket. 15" dia, 20" h. $600, North Carolina auction, fall 1985.

Cherokee Indians

The Cherokees in Tennessee and North Carolina as well as those in Oklahoma are well known for their excellent baskets and basketry items. Since they all started in the East and were taught basketry from childhood, there is little difference in the way they make baskets. Probably the biggest difference is that the Eastern group uses more grapevine whereas the Oklahoma group uses buck bush quite a bit.

The backbone of the Cherokee basket industry was, and still is, their oak-splint and cane baskets—the exquisitely colored baskets tinted with old vegetable dyes. Although new baskets are selling well, there is much more interest in the older ones. In fact, those made in the 1940s are commanding prices of $500 to $1,000 each. These are the so-called fancy baskets, not the regular work baskets. Many of the work baskets were made plain, that is, without color, although some were made with bright-colored weavers. All of these baskets have aged over the years to a beautiful patina, and some are almost as desirable today as the fancy or brightly colored baskets.

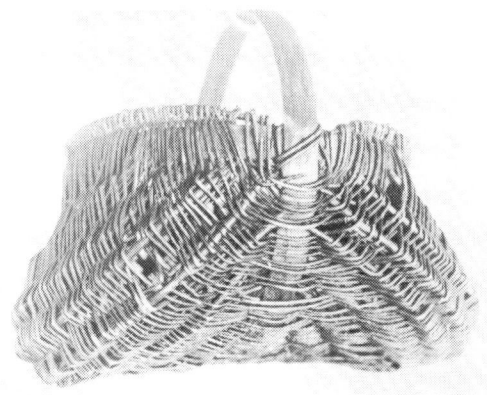

Vine basket, probably Oklahoma Cherokees. $150, Tennessee antique shop, fall 1985.

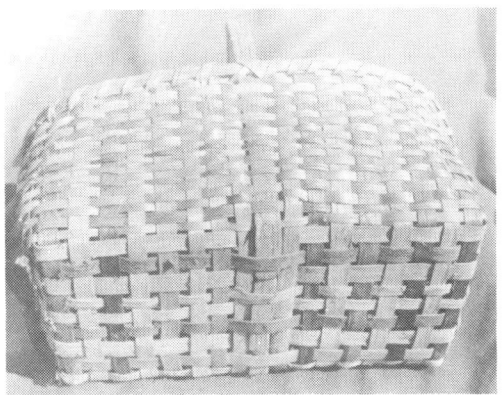

Oak-splint work basket with colored spokes and weavers. 13" w, 23" l, 18" o.h. $250, North Carolina antique shop, fall 1985.

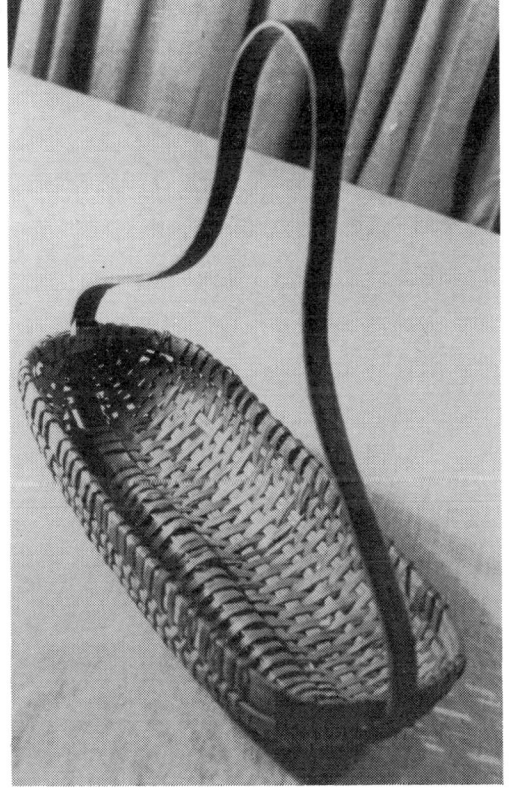

Oak-splint novelty basket, probably Cherokee. Private collection, NPA.

Unless the history is known, sometimes it is very difficult to ascertain whether an old basket, either work or fancy, was made by Indians or whites. This is especially true of the work baskets, since the Cherokees were a peaceful farming tribe who made and used baskets long before the white man arrived. The white settlers had also been making baskets in their native countries, and brought their skills with them.

The Indians and settlers probably exchanged basketmaking ideas. No doubt they incorporated the best of both methods into the baskets they have continued to make for centuries.

Chestnut Basket

This is not an American-made basket, yet chestnut baskets are showing up in American antique shops, shows, and malls. They were, and maybe still are, being used to ship chestnuts from Portugal—presumably to America, which would explain them being here. They are well-built with spokes as thick as one-half inch, and weavers over one-fourth inch thick. That makes a very heavy basket, and one that looks old. The empty basket weighs nine pounds, or about three times as much as a splint basket the same size. Several different sizes have been seen.

Chinese Wedding Baskets

Chinese wedding baskets have been made over a long period of time, and quite often, older examples will be found in the states. New ones are easily found as they are imported on a regular basis. New Chinese-made baskets can be found every place from specialty stores to discount houses. The newer baskets are a bit drab compared to the older ones with the gaily painted floral designs. They're made in a variety of sizes from 14 to 40 inches. The original use is elusive, but it's safe to assume that brides used them to take special things to their new homes. These baskets, with their three compartments, are useful today for holding anything from mail to sewing projects.

Chestnut shipping basket. 15" w, 18" l, 21" h. $55, New England antique show, fall 1986.

(left) Old wedding basket with top missing, $5, Maine antique shop, fall 1986; (right) new brown wedding basket, $25, Ohio gift shop, fall 1986.

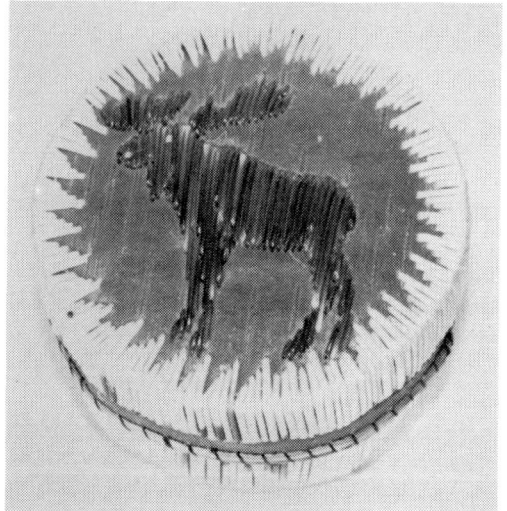

Birch-bark box with porcupine quill decoration. Unity College collection, NPA.

Chippewa Indians

Ojibwas, the original name for this tribe, was corrupted to Chippewa by some of the very first settlers, and in the ensuing years they became better known by that name rather than the original name.

Porcupine-quill decorated Chippewa-made box. 3" dia, 2" h. $85, Maine antique mall, fall 1986.

Beautifully designed, three-color Chitimacha basket. Private collection, NPA.

They lived too far north—from Maine to the Maritimes, through the Great Lakes area of Michigan and Wisconsin, and on into Minnesota, Canada, and parts of Alaska—to depend on agriculture as did so many other tribes. One of the reasons they became scattered over such a large area was their continuous search for better hunting and fishing grounds, and areas with an abundance of birch trees. Birch grows best in those areas, and it was essential to the making of not only their basketry items, but other things like canoes, containers for fish and game, and buckets for water, and it was needed to make the exquisite porcupine quill work for which they are justifiably proud. The Chippewas still do some porcupine quill work today, and they still use familiar things for designs.

Chitimacha Indians

Baskets were made in North America long before the white man came, but nowhere did it become such a fine art as among the Chitimachas. Throughout their long history they have been noted for their finely crafted and beautifully made baskets.

Another style Chitimacha basket. Private collection, NPA.

There is only one Chitimacha basketmaker still working, but chances of getting one of her new baskets is rather slim as she is two years behind on orders.

Pride in their heritage, which is exemplified in their basketry, along with the growing demand for their baskets has caused at least one of the older Chitimacha basketmakers to talk of returning to basketmaking.

Covered Chitimacha basket. Private collection, NPA.

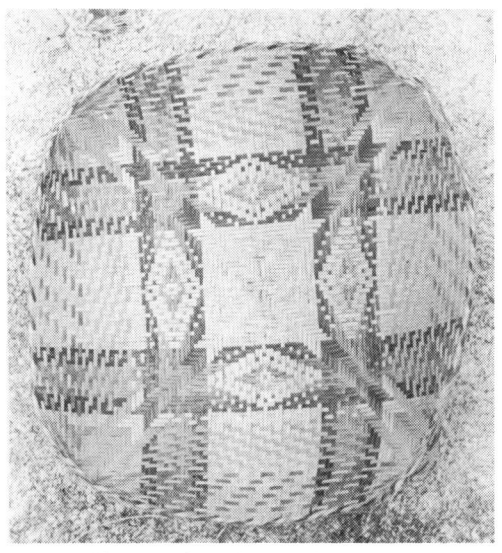

Large Chitimacha three-color tray. Private collection, NPA.

Chitimacha basketmaking is an art form that requires a great deal of skill. In fact, their baskets are not just baskets—they are objects of art, especially the double-woven baskets. *Double-woven* is a process that produces two baskets, one inside the other, with a perfect side both inside and out. The double-woven shares a single rim, and there is no visible place showing where the basket was started and stopped. Double weaving makes a strong, durable basket, and it can be watertight.

Although some rare examples of the old double weave can still be found, they're extremely scarce. On a trip through Louisiana and the Chitimacha reservation, we were unable to find one of their baskets offered for sale. Finally, we were able to photograph some in a private collection.

For generations, the art of basketry was passed down from mother to daughter, but eventually the younger children lost interest—it is a slow, time-consuming chore that doesn't pay that well.

Today, the one remaining Chitimacha basketmaker is selling her large double-woven baskets for as much as $2,000, but that is not a spectacular hourly rate when you consider it takes her approximately a month of 8- to 15-hour days to weave the basket. This doesn't include the time spent gathering the cane, or *piya,* as the Chitimachas call it, and the time spent preparing it.

Gathering the piya from the canebrakes along the bayous is a hot, sticky chore. There, the basketmaker selects the tallest and straightest stalks of the bamboo-like cane. She also searches for stalks with the longest joints, because too many joints have a way of disfiguring baskets. The cane, dozens and dozens of stalks, must be kept damp until it is time to split it. When the weaver gets down to the task of splitting the swamp cane, each stalk has to be split, and split again, until the strips are barely a half-inch wide. The smooth outside layer cane is peeled away from the pithy center with the basketmaker's hands and teeth. This leaves the inner white layer which is placed in the dew for a couple of weeks until the natural green bleaches out.

According to Faye Stouff, who still lives on the reservation, most of the basketmakers are using commercial dyes, but in the old days, the Chitimachas, like all other basketmakers, used vegetable dyes made from plants and roots growing around the the reservation. Gathering the dye materials required time and experience, and the actual dying, although not difficult, was time-consuming. To obtain the black that makes one of the dramatic colors in their baskets, the cane had to be boiled in a solution of black walnuts and walnut leaves for nine days. To obtain red, the Cherokees used bloodroot or puccoon; in Louisiana, the Chitimachas used the root of the dock plant, a plant they called *La Passiance*, for red. To obtain their third dramatic color, yellow, they used *powaac* root.

After the swamp cane was dyed and dried, another layer was peeled off, and then the basketmaker was ready to begin the long chore of weaving the basket—a chore that would keep her working for approximately 100 hours on a medium-sized single weave basket, or 300 to 400 hours on a large double-weave basket.

The Chitimachas are another tribe who have kept the names of the symbols used in their baskets. Designs copied from earlier baskets have little perch (fish) darting around, along with blackbirds' eyes, snake hearts, and turtles. Although these symbols are still used, their origin has been lost, but it had much to do with the Chitimachas' closeness with nature and their dependence on it.

Not only is the origin of the designs lost in the sea of antiquity, the Chitimachas no longer know why they only use the three brilliant colors—red, black, and yellow. These colors also fade with age, but not as severely as some others.

Collection of Choctaw baskets. Museum, NPA.

Choctaw Indians

The Choctaw Indians in Mississippi consider crafts to be a very old, perhaps the oldest, language. Any craft, they believe, allows the worker to express his or her opinions, dreams, and hopes, and if the work is good, it will last for many years—sometimes several lifetimes.

Oak-splint basketry has long been considered men's work among the Choctaws, while swamp-cane baskets were made by women. This is not to say the women don't make splint baskets and vice versa, but the majority of the work seems to be divided that way between the Choctaw men and women. The reason for that division is probably because oak splints were used to make work baskets, which had to be tough and strong, and cane baskets were fancier and easier to make.

Even the large burden baskets had to be as light as possible because the women used them. These baskets could be attached to a tumpline and worn across the head, and in that way could be carried for miles. In the old, days the Choctaw traders might walk all the way from the middle of

Old Choctaw cane basket. 12" dia, 14" h. $95, Mississippi antique mall, spring 1986.

New Choctaw cane basket. 10" dia, 13" h. $35, Choctaw reservation, spring 1986.

Old Choctaw cane egg basket. 10" dia, 13" h. $85, Mississippi antique mall, spring 1986.

New double-weave cane basket, Choctaw. 12" dia, 13" h. $250, Choctaw reservation, spring 1986.

Mississippi to New Orleans carrying a basket filled with things to sell or trade—things made or grown by the Indians, like herbs, nuts, and baskets.

The Choctaws have always made baskets, both oak-splint and cane, and today, they continue the tradition begun centuries ago. Some of the cane baskets are single-weave, others are double-weave—and just as always, they dye the cane to make designs in the baskets.

Today, the Choctaw reservation is filled with new industry, but the Choctaws continue to make baskets as they always have. Appreciation for their basketry, along with good prices, has had a bearing on this continued basketmaking. Twenty-five years ago, cane baskets were selling for under $5 unless they were very old and unusual; now, the going price for new ones is around $50 for a medium-size basket, and as high as $350 for a double-woven one.

Church-Offering Basket

In the past, many churches, especially rural churches, used collection or offering baskets. It was a long-handled basket that could be passed up and down the pews to collect the tithes of the parishoners. Church officials would pass the baskets up and down either side of the pews, holding the long-handled baskets in front of each person. Some of the baskets were lined with velvet to soften the noise when change was dropped in them.

Clematis

Clematis is fast becoming a cultivated plant, but there was a time when much of it grew wild and was used frequently in basketmaking. It's a woody climbing plant of the *crowfoot* family and is very desirable as a garden plant, due to its large, brightly colored blue, pink, purple, and white flowers. Clematis was used both for spokes and weavers, and was sometimes mixed with other vines to make baskets.

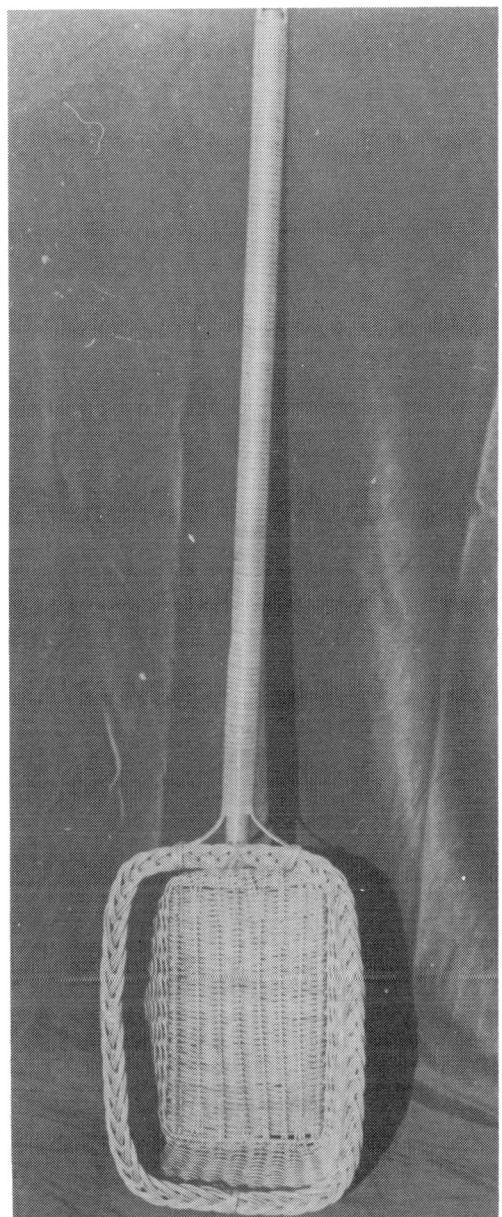

Rattan church-offering basket. 10" w, 13½" l, 45" l, including handle. $36, Maine antique shop, fall 1986.

Willow clothes hamper. 18" w, 24" l, 24" h. $35, Rhode Island antique shop, fall 1986.

Clothes Hamper

Hampers have long been a favorite place to store one's clothing, both clean and dirty. Actually, the first mention of a hamper—or what was later identified as a hamper—was in the will of a man who died in 1675. Among his choice possessions was one "Wikker Flasket."

Man has long made woven hampers. The first ones were made of willow, or as the man described it—wikker—while others were made of various splints. Most of the early hampers were made by hand, but later, the majority were factory-made. During the past quarter century, woven hampers have suffered a decline in popularity because of built-in storage spaces in modern homes.

Factory-made splint hamper. 13" w, 18" l, 27" h. $5, Maine auction, fall 1986.

Clothespin basket with plywood bottom. 12" dia. $3, Maine barn sale, fall 1986.

Clothespin Basket

This is not a basket *for* clothespins, but rather a basket made *of* clothespins. This intricately fashioned basket was made 40 years ago by a man who used regular spring-type wooden clothespins to make this basket for his small granddaughter.

Cochineal

Cochineal is a scale insect *(coccus cacti)* that is a native of the warmer climates of America. It can be found in several species of cactus, especially the Indian fig tree. Red dye for baskets was made from the bodies of the females.

Old coiled-straw basket. 8" dia, 20" o.h. $25, Maine antique shop, fall 1986.

Coiled basket of unknown material and origin. 17" dia, 19½" h. $35, Maine auction, fall 1986.

Coiled-Straw Baskets

This type basketry may have originated in Germany, where it is believed to have been first used to make bee hives, but it was perfected by the Germans who moved to Pennsylvania. They used the coiled straw to make containers and baskets for their chores. Rye was the first straw used for these baskets, and later, the Pennsylvania Germans used whatever straw was available. These baskets are still made by a few of the old basketmakers, and even some of the old baskets can still be found.

Coiling

Unlike the woven basket that has spokes and weavers, the coiled basket is made from one long, flexible rod made of tightly coiled cattails, rush, willow, or corn husk, or any of a number of other materials. The rod or coil may be covered completely with raffia, yucca, palm leaves, or other materials, and then sewn together at intervals. Or, it can be sewn together not only to hold it, but to form a design.

Small baskets can be made either by coiling or weaving, but coiling is recommended for tiny ones. Like the woven basket, the coiled one can be made in any shape—round, square, oval, oblong—but it is best suited to the round size.

Coil Wrap

Some of the people making baskets during the first decades of this century used a method called *coil wrap* in which they used leftover yarn and threads to cover grass, or rush, to make coil basketry items. A few of these can still be found and are usually displayed with other baskets. During the past few years, this method of basketry has been revived, but with a new twist. Now the coils are generally made of large scraps of fabric and are wrapped with other colorful strips of fabric.

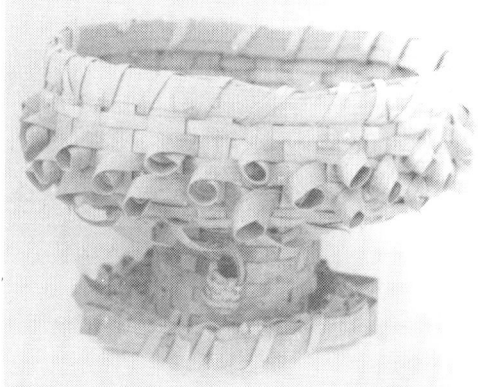

Ash-splint woven compote. 10" dia, 7" h. $25, Maine antique mall, fall 1986.

Compote, Woven

Compotes woven of various basketry materials are seen occasionally. The workmanship on some is excellent, while others, although made with much fancier designs, still lack skilled workmanship. The illustration is an example of the latter. For one thing, the splints are not top quality, and they are too wide. There are too many decorations—like the curliques and miniature baskets hanging around the sides. The idea would have worked better with smaller splints; nevertheless, it's a beautiful piece of primitive basketry. Some of the weavers were dyed green, others red, but through the years they have faded almost completely. The miniature woven baskets hanging around the bottom of the bowl measure one inch in diameter, and are two inches in overall height. It was covered with black cobwebs when found, indicating it had been stored for many years.

Coralberry

Another name for Indian currant. See Indian Currant.

Ladies' corn husk hat. Pike Museum, NPA.

Corn Husk Basketry

Corn husk basketry has been called a southern craft. If it was strictly a southern craft it would be called corn shuck, as that is the common southern name for the outside husk or shuck of an ear of corn.

Outside the South, Northern Indians made corn husk masks to be used in planting and harvesting celebrations. They may have also made other basketry items with the corn husks such as hats, fans, mats, and bags, as well as baskets. The husks or shucks were twisted and used to make seats or *bottomchairs,* hearth brooms, and mops.

In the South, mops were made by boring holes in a small oblong piece of wood and attaching a handle. The corn husks were twisted and then pulled through the holes leaving over half the husks to form the mop.

Surprisingly, corn husks could be used in a number of ways to make basketry items. They could be braided and the braids sewn together in circles or squares to make mats. They could also be folded into small pointed pieces and sewn on cardboard or buckram to make hats. Although it was seldom done, they could be woven on the old looms to make table mats or place mats, or used as the base for coiled basketry. Sometimes they were rolled into a hard core, wrapped with raffia, and used to make the coiled Indian baskets (described in various instruction books on basketry published around the turn of the century).

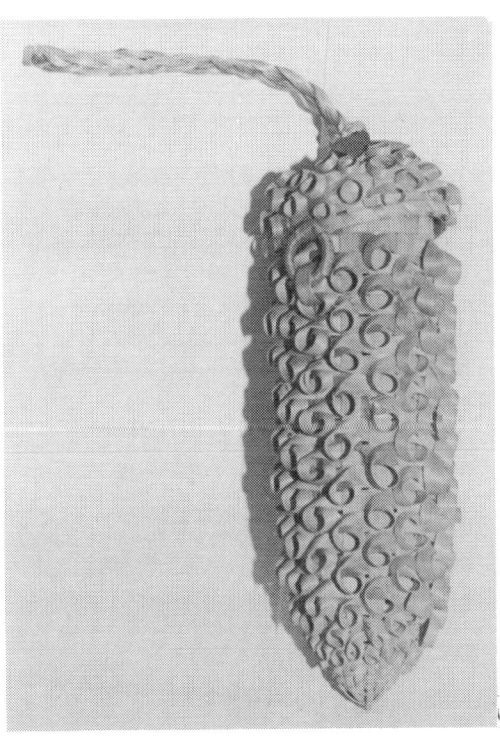

Ash and sweet-grass basket shaped like an ear of corn. Unity College collection, NPA.

Corn-Shaped Basketry

During the heyday of basketry souvenir making, the Passamaquoddies began making baskets that resembled various foods. No doubt, others joined in, but credit for the beginning of this type of basketry is attributed to the Passamaquoddy tribe.

One of the most attractive "food baskets" is the one shaped like an ear of corn. It's very realistic and even has silks. It's woven of tough, but flexible, paper-thin ash splints with circles to represent the individual grains. The top has a sweet-grass handle, a sort of trademark of the Passamaquoddy-made food baskets. Pumpkin baskets were dyed orange and acorn baskets were dyed green, but if the corn basket was dyed yellow, the color has faded. It is the natural golden color of ash.

Corn-Sifting Baskets

Most, if not all, southern tribes of Indians, and some whites, made corn-sifting baskets of cane. The bottom basket was solidly and closely woven to hold the corn meal once it had been separated from the husk. The top loosely woven basket allowed the meal to sift through, and it would later be used to make cornbread or some other dish requiring corn meal.

Pair of corn-sifting baskets of swamp cane. 12" square, 3" h. $75, Cousatta reservation, spring 1986.

Oak-splint cotton basket. 18" dia, 19" h. $75, Texas antique shop, spring 1986.

Cotton Basket

Shortly after the settlers arrived in the southern states they began to grow cotton. Until mills could be built in the north, the cotton was shipped to England to be made into fabric. There was a problem with seed removal, but Eli Whitney solved that one with his gin. This really paved the way for the growth of cotton.

To harvest the fields of cotton the pickers had to go in with long osnaburg cotton sacks they filled by picking the fluffy white bolls—one at a time. Rather than let the pickers lose valuable time walking long distances to a waiting wagon or to the barn, the grower made or bought numerous oak-splint cotton baskets that were placed at either end of the row, sometimes in the middle of long rows. Each picker or family of pickers had a basket.

The baskets of cotton were weighed at night, and then the pickers were paid for their labors. Cotton baskets of approximately the same size were never weighed separately, as it was an accepted fact that large cotton baskets weighed eight pounds; therefore, eight pounds were automatically deducted from the total of each basket of cotton.

Unfortunately, the days of the cotton basket were numbered. Shortly after the turn of the present century the basket began to be replaced by cotton spreads, large squares of osnaburg. It was much easier to empty cotton sacks on the spreads, as they didn't have to pack the cotton in as they did in the baskets, and the spreads were easy to move and store. By this time, cotton was no longer king in the south as farming was becoming more diversified, and the demise of the cotton basket didn't seem to matter. In a few years it would all be replaced by the mechanical cotton picker.

But the old cotton baskets continued to be used around the farm for a few chores—like harvesting corn, potatoes, and cabbages. A few of the old baskets have survived. These baskets are not as popular as other types. Today they're used for wood for the fireplace or for magazines.

Cottonwood

One of several trees of the genus Populus. Grows mostly in the eastern part of the country, and is called cottonwood because of the flowers that have scaly spikes, no petals, and has cotton-like tufts on the seeds. The flower closely resembles those on the willow and birch, and like the willow the shoots can be used in basketry. They are tough and flexible which makes them perfect for either spokes or weavers. The shoots or rods may be split several times to make fine splints for weaving. Flexible cottonwood shoots have also been used as the foundation for coiled baskets, and it is said that many Indian gambling baskets had cottonwood foundations.

Coushatta Indians

The Coushatta tribe was well established in America when DeSoto arrived. Records show DeSoto and his men kidnapped the chief and some of the tribe leaders but released them shortly thereafter. Following that brief and terrifying experience, the Coushattas began a peaceful co-existence with the white man that lasted through

New pine needle basket with Indian head on top. 4" dia, 6" h. $15, Coushatta reservation, spring 1986.

New pine needle basket with open-work design. 9" dia, 12" o.h., $23, Coushatta reservation, spring 1986.

Another style new pine needle basket. 10" dia, 11½" o.h. $25, Coushatta reservation, spring 1986.

New vase and covered box made of pine needles. Vase $9, box $12, Coushatta reservation, spring 1986.

Small pine needle covered box (new) made by 80-year-old man. 3" dia, 2" h. $5, Coushatta reservation, 1986.

most of the 17th century. Then in 1783, treaties were broken and wars broke out in which thousands of warriors were lost, and the Coushattas had to give up millions of acres of their land.

It became apparent they would have to search for a place where they could live in peace. Late in the 18th century, one of the Coushatta leaders, Red Shoes (who was known as King of the Alabamas and Coushattas) lead a band of 80 to 100 men to the banks of the Red River in Louisianna. Several other moves followed, and by 1884, most of the Coushattas had settled near Elton, Louisianna in Allen Parish where they remain today.

The Coushatta have always made exquisite baskets and basketry items. A historical marker standing on the highway that leads to the reservation says the following: "Coushatta Indians, three miles north, is a tribe that migrated in 1795 to Louisiana from Alabama. Name means 'white reed brake'; Choushatta town in Red River parish named for them. Noted for basket handicraft." Indeed they are noted for their fine baskets and have justified their name Choushatta or white reed brake.

Some Coushattas still make the swamp-cane or reed baskets, but today they are best known for their coiled pine needle baskets. Not only do they make baskets using pine needles, but effigies of the animals they are familiar with, the ones that live near them. Both men and women make baskets. They wrap the pine needles in colored raffia to make crawfish, ducks, chickens, armadillos, owls, and turtles. They also make a small covered pine needle box or basket with an Indian head on top. Black raffia makes the hair while small black stitches form the eyes. Red forms the lips.

Originally, the Coushattas were known as Koastis.

Willow cradle with missing hood. $125, Maine auction, fall 1986.

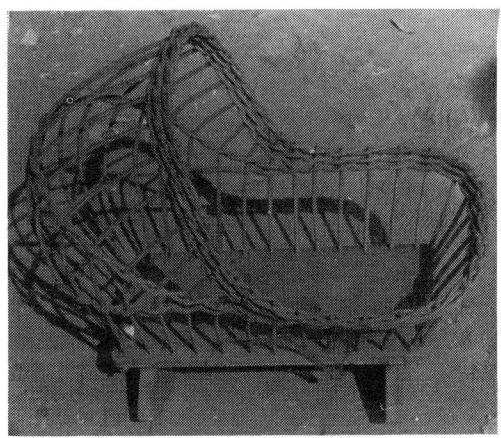

Late wicker doll cradle. $35, Tennessee auction, fall 1985.

Cradle, Baby

When a cradle appears in an older picture and painting the cradle is often made of willow. At one time, willow was the only material used to make baby cradles. Willow is flexible and softer than oak splints. Later cradles were made of oak splints.

Strangely, parents seldom, if ever, took the cradle with them when going to church or socials. Instead, they would put the baby in a large laundry basket which apparently was easier than trying to carry the cradle.

Cradle, Doll

About a century ago one of the few jobs most girls could look forward to was that of homemaker. Knowing that, parents trained them well. They often played with dolls and in playhouses. This accounts for the large number of *housekeeping toys* like doll cradles. These doll cradles were made of oak and ash splint, and willow. During the 1920s, a cheaper version of the wicker was made—today, it is quite collectible.

Cradle, Miniature

Since man first learned to weave willow, grasses, splints and other materials into useful items, he has made cradles. Sometimes for the baby, other times for his children's dolls, and oftentimes just to test his skills and ability.

Old oak-splint doll cradle, hood missing. 9" w, 17" l, 6½" h. $35, Maine auction, fall 1986.

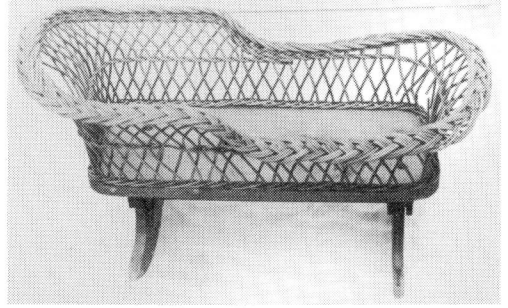

Old wicker doll cradle. 10" w, 20" l, 10" h. $95, Alabama Tag Sale, spring 1986.

Most of the small ash-splint cradles were made by four Indian tribes, the Penobscots, Passamaquoddies, Maliseets, and Micmacs. Each of these groups made cradles to be sold to tourists, the visitors coming into Maine during the summers a century or so ago. Today, these miniatures are avidly sought by both miniature and novelty collectors.

Vine as well as fine oak-splint examples are known, and the latter is believed to have been made by both the Cherokees and the settlers in the Great Smoky and Ozark mountains.

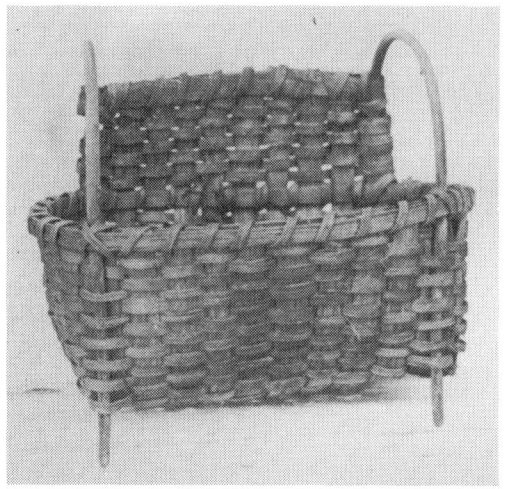

This tiny oak-splint piece is called a miniature cradle by the owner. Private collection, NPA.

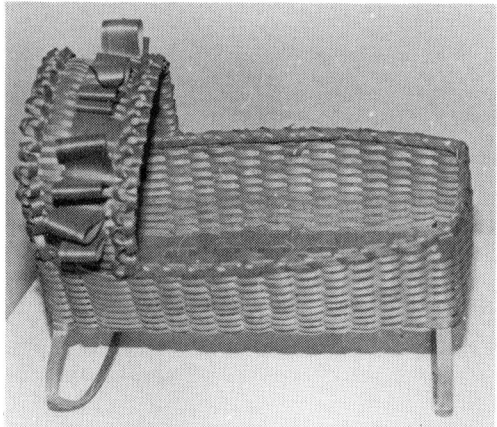

Old ash-splint hooded miniature cradle. Unity College collection, NPA.

*Different style ash-splint miniature cradle (left) 7½" l, 6" h, **$56**, antique mall in Maine, fall 1986. Late cradle, rockers missing, 6" l, 5½" h, **$15**, same mall, fall 1986.*

*Pine needle crawfish. 9" l, 2¼" w. **$18**, Coushatta reservation, spring 1986.*

Crawfish, Pine Needle

Louisiana has long been famous for its crawfish, so it was only natural that the Coushatta Indians would make a replica of one using pine needles and red raffia. It is very realistic looking and has a small container on the back that qualifies it as basketry. The Coushattas are so skilled in basketry, the 1 × 2 inch lid fits perfectly.

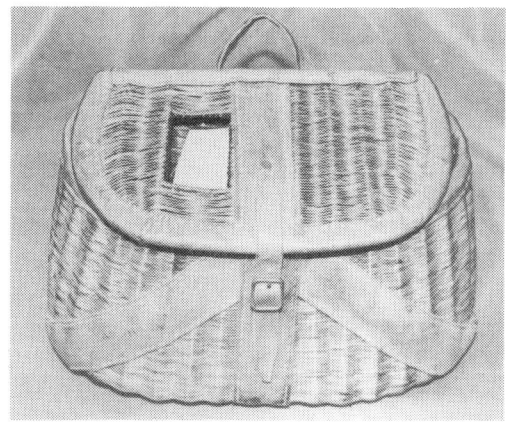

Creel with leather trim. Private collection, NPA.

Creel

A *creel* is a woven basket used to hold the fisherman's catch until he is ready to go home. Some are primitively made while others are elaborate. They're all odd-shaped little baskets— some plain, others with genuine leather trim.

A decade ago, there was little demand for used creels; thus, you could buy one for less than $5. But there is much more demand now and it's not unusual to see a

Crudely made ash-splint creel. 7" w, 11" l, 12½" h. $28, Maine antique show, Winter 1987.

dozen or more creels displayed in one booth at the larger antique shows. They're usually used for decorative purposes, either to hang on the wall or place on a desk or table. The plain ones are gaining popularity as containers for houseplants.

Crocheted Basket

Needleworkers have always crocheted some baskets, but the current popularity of baskets in general has caused many more to be made recently. This is a good example of how baskets can be made of any material, using a variety of methods.

Crooked Knife

Type of knife used to cut splints for making baskets.

Covered Baskets

Covers and lids were made for all kinds of baskets depending on the basket's use as well as the whim of the maker. In most areas, in the early days, baskets had covers to keep out the mice, rats, and squirrels. That also explains why so many of the storage-type baskets were made of thicker splints—it was more difficult for the rodents to chew through them.

Sewing baskets, sewing stands, pie baskets, lunch baskets, and picnic baskets usually always had covers or lids.

Covered ash-splint basket. Unity College collection, NPA.

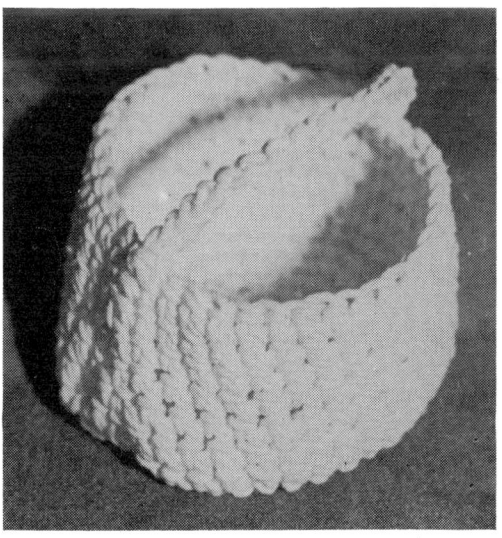

Crocheted basket. 2" dia, 2½" o.h. $2, New England flea market, fall 1986.

Three ash-splint baskets: (bottom) 14" dia, 10" h, $45, Maine antique show; (middle) 12" dia, 10" h, $50; (top) 6" dia, 3½" h, $15, same show, fall 1986.

Covered ash-splint basket. 8" dia, 4" h. $35, Massachusetts antique shop, fall 1986.

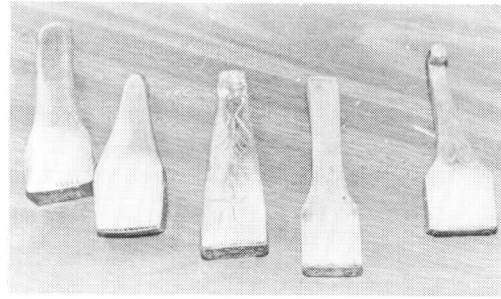

Five assorted cutters for ash splint. Note the carved design on the handle in the middle. Private collection, NPA.

Plain ash-splint pie basket. 11" dia, 5" h, $17, Maine auction, fall 1986.

Cutters for Ash Splint

Makers of ash-splint baskets had to be inventive. They not only had to devise a comb to be used on the sweet grass, but had to make cutters and knives to split the ash strips into assorted sizes. They made a wooden handle onto which they attached sharpened springs or wires from a clock; some used strong piano wires. The cutters were grasped by the handle and slowly and smoothly pulled along the length of a strip of ash. Depending on the cutter used, they would have anything from a very fine to maybe a half-inch wide strip, and they could cut from 6 to 12 strips at one time.

Devil's Claw

Devil's claw or *devil's horn* are the common names for the herbaceous plant *martynia*, named for the Cambridge University botanist John Martyn (1699–1768). The plant has clammy smelling leaves, large violet blossoms, and dark green pods.

The pods are the only part of the plant used. They are gathered and split into fine strips to add color to baskets. Several tribes use devil's claw in their basketry, but the Papagos use it most often. Since the color of the dried pods can vary from dark gray to black, they're usually dyed to get an even color. The dyed devil's claw is then bound in with yucca to cover the willow, or bear grass foundation. Using devil's claw involves more work; therefore, baskets with this decoration are higher priced, sometimes twice as much as plain yucca baskets.

Devil's Horn

Another name for the herbaceous plant martynia. See Devil's Claw.

Dish Drainer Basket

This basket is large enough to hold dishes and may or may not have been used as a dish drainer. It's made of an unknown, pithy-type vine. The larger-sized vines were used for spokes or standards and the braided border, while the smaller ones were used for weavers.

Double-woven Choctaw basket. 10" dia, 13" h. $200, Choctaw reservation, spring 1986.

Double-Woven Baskets

Many of the early baskets were double woven so they could be waterproofed. Then, as water containers came into use, the need for waterproof baskets decreased. Several tribes, especially the Cherokee and Choctaw, made some double-woven baskets for their own use and for sale.

As basket collecting grows in popularity, basketmakers are quickly reverting to double woven. They are made of swamp or river cane, and are dyed in several colors.

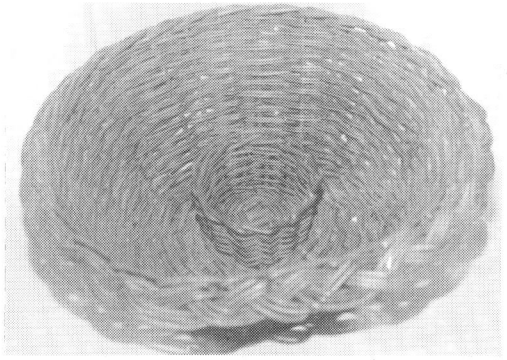

Vine dish-drainer basket, 13½" dia, 5" h. $35, private home, fall 1986.

Double-woven Choctaw with different design. 12" dia, 14" h. $250, Choctaw reservation, spring 1986.

Basket with double-wrapped rim.

Double-Wrapped Rim

To make a double wrap or "X" binding on the top or the rim of splint baskets, the weaver went around the top in one direction, then reversed the procedure for the second time around. When completed, the top of the basket was covered with a double row of binding making it very strong and sturdy. Collectors usually prefer double-wrapped rims.

Drawing Horse

Same as shaving horse. See Shaving Horse.

Draw Knife

A tool with a very sharp blade with two handles: A sort of miniature two-man saw with a smooth blade, it is used for making splints and to cut and smooth off the rough places.

Dress Hats, Caps

The finely woven hats and caps made and worn by both Indian men and women, could more rightly be described as *skull caps* of a sort.

Most Indians wore hats at one time or another, some to protect themselves from rain and sun, others to alleviate some of the pressure from the tumpline. The *tumpline* was a head strap of sorts that was attached to a burden basket. The basket was hung on the back and the tumpline placed across the head. The hats and caps served as a kind of protection.

The Hupas made lovely woven hats and caps as did other tribes, including the Karoks and the Yuroks. The Utes also made hats, but of a coarser texture. The Haidas made a hat with a flaring brim. These hats and caps are often mistaken for bowls.

Eel Traps

Both Indians and Pilgrims enjoyed eating eels, and they shared practical ways of catching them. One of the most primitive methods was treading the eels out of brooks and streams using bare feet, and then catching them with bare hands.

They also made eel traps, which were necessary in order to catch a large number of eels. The Indians were quite skilled at this form of basketry—they had had more experience than the Pilgrims with the materials in the area.

Like all handmade items, the traps were made to fit the needs of the user. Small traps were used in shallow streams while the large ones were used in the ocean. Regardless of where they were used, the design of the traps was the same—a more or less cone-shaped apparatus with one or two cone-shaped inserts inside.

The large traps were anchored on the ocean floor with a buoy to identify the spot, and bait was placed inside the trap to attract the eels. Once inside, the eel was unable to get out as the top of the trap was covered with some sort of bag or stopper. When a fisherman pulled up the trap, he simply uncovered the top allowing the eels to swim out and into his boat.

The eel trap shown in the illustration was made by the Wampanoag Indians. This one is made of cedar roots because it was believed to be the longest lasting material for traps.

Finely woven old Hupa hat. 7" dia, 3" h. $250, Massachusetts antique shop, fall 1986.

Woven dryer with dowel type frame. 16" by 19" w, 2½" h. $45, Maryland antique mall, fall 1986.

Dryer, Woven

This woven, handmade dryer may have been used to dry apples, but doubtfully so unless the apples were cut into large pieces. It could have been used to dry other things or other fruits. Beans were usually strung to dry, but it's possible someone decided to try this method.

*Cedar-root eel trap made by Wampanoags. 6" dia top, 19" dia bottom, 6' 9" h. **$210**, Maine antique show, fall 1986.*

Bottom of eel trap showing first insert.

*Choctaw cane egg basket. 10" dia, 13" h. **$75**, Mississippi antique shop, 1985.*

Basket similar to those used in the mountains to take eggs on horseback.

Square oak-splint Deep South egg basket. 8" square, 13" o.h. $55, Atlanta antique show, 1985.

Buttocks or gizzard egg basket. 10" dia, 12" h. $150, Kentucky antique shop, 1985.

Egg Basket

A variety of styles and types of egg baskets were used in different places. Throughout most of the Midwest, the Ozarks, the Appalachians, and some of the border states, the *gizzard* or *buttocks* basket was known as the *egg basket*. Further south, both the white and black men made square and round oak-splint baskets for eggs. The southern Indians, especially the Choctaws, made a pretty, round cane egg basket. In the northeast, there wasn't a special basket just for eggs.

But baskets of one kind or another were used universally, if not for gathering and taking the eggs to the store, then for storing them in the home. There were also smaller baskets that resembled the hen basket that was used in parts of Kentucky and Tennessee. The basket's flat sides fit well against the horse's neck when one had to take the eggs to the store on horseback.

In some areas, these baskets were used for gathering and storing eggs, especially large duck, geese, and turkey eggs. Notice the crudely carved duck decoy in front.

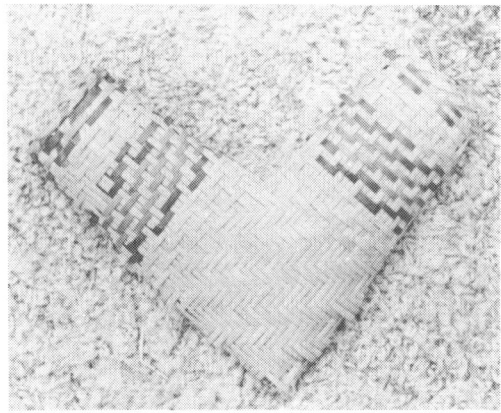

Chitimacha-made cane elbow basket, 16" w, 14" l. Private collection, NPA.

Elbow Basket

Originally, the elbow basket was made to keep valuables. It was carried on the arm like a purse and hung on a wall when not in use.

But, as most basketmakers and collectors know, baskets are used for a multitude of purposes, often not the purposes for which the baskets were made, as was the case of the elbow basket, shown here. The finely split cane basket was photographed in the home of a Chitimacha basketmaker who said she made it especially for her son when he was a young boy. It was used as a place to keep his toothbrush and toothpaste.

Elm

Both elm splints and roots have been used in basketry. Like any other basket material, makers used whatever was most suitable and most plentiful in the area. Elm trees seem to be more plentiful in Wisconsin and the surrounding areas. For that reason the Winnebagos and Chippewas seem to have used more elm in their basketry.

Embroidered Baskets

Several craft people have been successful with cross-stitched (embroidered) designs on the new loosely woven basketry items such as flat bowls, mats, trays, and fans. The weaving has to be even for best results. The smaller, more tightly woven pieces can be used as long as there is enough space between the spokes and weavers for the thread. Either fewer strands or smaller thread must be used on these baskets. Rug and left-over sweater yarns can be used on the looser-woven baskets.

There are numerous new bamboo items for sale in gift and discount stores. These can be converted from mundane pieces to one-of-a-kind basketry items by cross-stitching designs on them, much like those stitched on fabric.

English Ivy

English Ivy either grows wild or can be cultivated. In basketmaking, the larger vines are used for spokes and the smaller ones for weavers.

Eskimo Baskets

The word *Eskimo* was coined back in 1611 by a Jesuit. He had heard the Alaskan people referred to as *eskimantsik* by the neighboring Indians, and he translated that to Eskimo. At the time, the Eskimos called themselves *Inuit*, which is plural of *inuk* or man.

Even then, the Eskimos were making baskets. They had no other containers, so baskets were essential. With their many years of experience, it's only natural they

Yupik Eskimo basket, seal gut decoration. 8" h, 5" dia. $130, Alaska Native Arts and Crafts outlet, fall 1986.

laying on seal gut over the already-sewn stitches. Before, colors were obtained from alder bark and berries, and willow, but like basketmakers all over the country, they too are beginning to use commercial dyes.

Most still use specific shapes, designs, and styles that are characteristic of particular Eskimo villages. One of the best known is the small, Hooper-Bay shaped ginger jar.

Older factory-made picnic basket. 8" w, 13" l, 15" o.b. $12.50, Maine auction, spring 1987.

would make excellent baskets, and they have another advantage over other basketmakers—their winters are so long they can make plenty of them.

For their best baskets, the Eskimos go out on the tundra and along the shores of Alaska's Bering Sea where they gather a type of tough, but pliable, beach grass. During the late summer, the grasses are carefully selected, and then bleached and cured. The grass will be used during the long winter.

They also gather tundra and rye grass that covers the southwestern coast of Alaska to make the Yupik coiled baskets. The foundation for the coils is usually made from a bundle of grass; then, the stitches spiral around the foundation with each stitch interlocking the coil beneath it. At one time, the Eskimos decorated their baskets with animal parts, feathers, beads, and other objects. Now, their decorations consist mostly of sewing in dyed grass or

Smaller, solid-top picnic basket. 6" w, 10" l, 11" o.b. $18, Maine auction, fall 1986.

Factory-Made Baskets

Contrary to popular belief, factory-made baskets are almost completely handmade—the 46 individual hand operations are carried out by individuals on an assembly-type operation.

Older double-handled laundry basket, factory-made. 18" w, 24" l, 17" o.h. $25, Maine estate auction, fall 1986.

Old, small factory-made basket. $25, Tennessee auction, 1985.

Small, round, decorated factory-made basket, 4" dia. 8" h. $15, Maine estate auction, fall 1986.

Sidney Gage and Company—better known as Basketville—Putney, Vermont, describes the factory there as "the largest manufacturer of handmade baskets in the United States." They are said to produce the best baskets that can be made using assembly-line manufacturing. The same family has owned the factory since 1842 with the fourth generation now in charge. Some of their earlier-made baskets have already reached antique status.

Making baskets under factory conditions is not much different from making them at home—only the operation is larger with as many labor saving devices as possible.

They begin with the same knot-free ash and oak splints that have been cut to size. Just as the individual basketmaker must soften the wood before cutting the splints, so does the factory, but they must do it quickly as workers may be waiting on materials; therefore, they use vats of hot water. The splints are cut by hand with draw knives much like those used by individuals. The difference in the factory is that there may be a half-dozen men cutting splints at any one time. The splints are then treated with steam or hot water to make them pliable enough to fit the basket forms, and again, large amounts are treated at one time as there are many workers using them.

When the splints are ready, they're given to the worker who will weave the bottom of the basket. The bottoms are woven rapidly and placed in a rack for the weavers who will shape and weave them over the forms or molds.

The baskets are then sent by conveyor to the workers who will fasten bands around the top and attach handles. Lids may be attached to those requiring them. Some lids are painted and decorated before attaching.

All types of baskets are made in the factories, but usually they're of wide splint like picnic baskets; market baskets; baskets for backpacking, sewing, and laundry; and baskets for mail, condiments, wine, berries, garden, harvest, pies and cake, and ladies handbags.

Mountain-made oak splint (left) and round ash splint and sweet grass (right). About $7.50 each in areas where they are made.

Fans

Prior to the invention of electric fans, and long before air conditioning was a gleam in the inventor's eye, people used fans, the kind they worked themselves in an effort to stay cool. They spent most of each Sunday in church, and the same church that could be so cold in winter could be as miserably hot in summer. So the communicants used small tin or soapstone heaters in winter, and fans in summer.

Later, there would be cardboard advertising fans, but in those early days, the ladies and some of the gentlemen depended on Oriental fans if they could afford them. If they couldn't, or just wanted to save money, they made their own fans. In the South, they made fans of palm leaves; in the mountains, they used oak splints; and in the Northeast, round fans made of ash splints were a favorite. Oftentimes, the latter was made of a combination of ash splints and sweet grass. The fragrance of the sweet grass would last for years and was very pleasant when fanned across one's face.

Some of the fans were works of art, because the maker put forth her best efforts, knowing all the other ladies in church would see her workmanship on the finished product. Other beautiful fans were made by Indians of the Northeast, to be sold to the summer visitors who would use them as they sat on the porches around the big hotels.

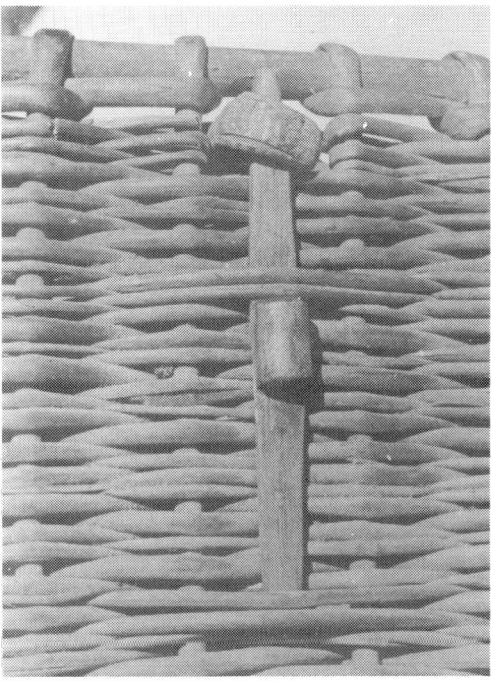

A primitive fastener on a picnic basket.

Fasteners on Basket Covers

Ways of fastening basket lids and covers vary with the whims and ability of the maker. Some used rings made of the same material as the basket. It was made to fasten over a protruding woven piece. Others made a wide weave in the lid and carved a crude fastener to put in it. Some of the baskets have no fasteners—the weight of the lid holds it in place.

Ash-splint feather basket. 13½" dia, 12" o.h. $135, Massachusetts antique mall, fall 1986.

Feather Basket

Before there were ready-made mattresses, each household made its own. These were usually made from corn shucks, straw, or feathers. Feathers were plentiful, but since much work was involved in securing them, they soon became a status symbol—a homemaker was known and praised for the number of feather beds she owned. Some beds were stuffed so full of feathers, they might be 12 to 15 inches high when sunned and fluffed.

The homemaker deserved praise for her feather beds as feathers weren't as easy to obtain as one might think. Duck, chicken, turkey, and eagle feathers could be used, but goose down was the most desirable. It was also the most difficult to acquire—naturally, the geese, which were raised for producing down, were very upset about having their feathers plucked. A contraption was made to fit over the goose's head during plucking, so the plucker had to hold a basket over the goose's head while plucking, as well as deposit the feathers and down in the feather basket.

The feather basket was made to help as much as possible. The lid was fastened around the handles so it could be raised and lowered easily, without being knocked off. Feather baskets were made of all kinds of splints, but the most desirable ones now are the ones made of ash splints.

Rattan basket and tray with plywood bottom. Both made in the Fifties. $3 to $5 each.

Fifties Basketry

Through the years, basketry has experienced revivals, and it has survived slumps when only the very dedicated continued to make a few baskets.

There was a major revival around the turn of the century, another around 1938, and still another in the 1950s, with the present revival overshadowing anything that has happened before.

The Fifties revival wasn't nearly as strong as the present revival. Boy and Girl Scout troops were taught the basics of basketmaking, church groups taught the fundamentals to children in summer Bible classes, and adult members made basketry items to be sold in fall bazaars.

And, it was common, during that time, for young housewives to get together to make baskets, trays, and other basketry items for their homes.

With the increased interest in things from the Fifties, it's not surprising that some of those baskets are showing up in antique shops, malls, and yard sales.

Old finely woven miniature splint basket. 3" dia, 1¾" h. $50, Maine antique show, winter 1987.

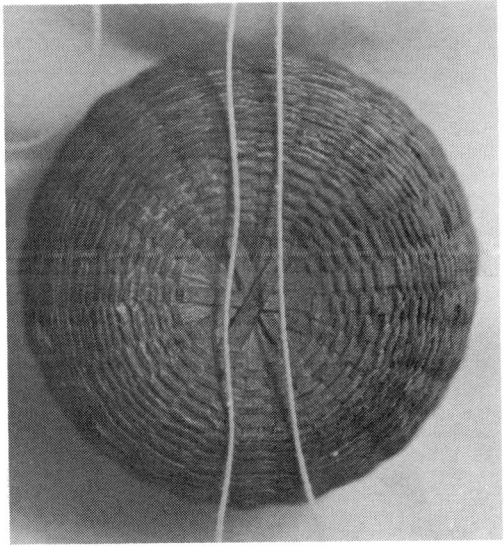

Same basket with small thread for comparison with splints.

Finely Woven Baskets

The weaving of baskets could very appropriately be classified into about half a dozen categories. There are several classes of loosely woven baskets just as there are several types of finely woven ones. The majority of baskets will have average weaving, but those with super-fine splints woven closely are hard to find.

The majority of the finely woven baskets are small, as it takes much more time to make a small fine-woven basket than a large, average weave basket.

Since the actual number of finely woven baskets is much less than other types, they are more difficult to find. The finely woven baskets were probably made as gifts or when the basketmaker was experimenting. Makers were probably lucky to get 25 cents for them.

Finishes for Baskets

Many of the new baskets made today, especially the pine needles made by the white basketmakers, are finished with a solution of lacquer that makes them very stiff and hard. They are totally unlike the soft, flexible pine needle baskets made by the Indians. Through the years, some of the basketmakers have varnished, painted, and lacquered their new baskets, but the majority were left natural.

Now that baskets are so much a part of modern decor—they're used in the home rather than the pantry or barn—a finish might be nice in some cases, but generally they are nicer when left natural. Some collectors claim a finish keeps them from becoming dry and brittle.

To avoid brittleness, some basket collectors put their baskets outside on a regular basis, letting them stay out in the rain for a week or so, while others prefer spraying them with varnish or lacquer. Another method that is chosen by many to preserve and add life to their baskets is to give them an application of about three parts linseed oil to one part turpentine.

If none of the above appeals to you, it does add life to baskets to take them outside annually and spray them with a water hose.

Firewood basket being used as a magazine basket in a room of wicker. Private collection, NPA.

Fancy firewood basket painted white. 18" w, 21" h. $55, Texas antique shop, 1985.

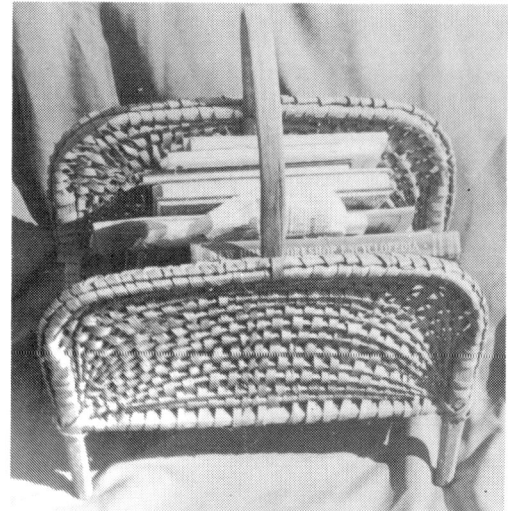

Oak-splint firewood basket. Private collection, NPA.

Natural woven-splint firewood basket. 20" l, 19" h. $10, Maine antique mall, fall 1986.

Firewood Baskets

As late as 1925 many homes did all their cooking and heating with wood-burning stoves (this was especially true in rural homes). Even when oil, gas, and electricity became available many continued to use wood—it was plentiful, cheap, and they were accustomed to it.

Once the wood was cut and brought home, it was stored in barns and sheds around the house until it was needed. Then, it was carried into the house where it was put in woodboxes. For the parlor, that might only be used once a week; on Sunday, a woven firewood basket was used. It might be factory-made or handmade. Handmade firewood baskets were, and still are, the most desirable. The logs were placed neatly in the firewood basket to be used in the fancy parlor heater.

When other types of heat were finally accepted, the firewood baskets were relegated to the basement where they were discovered by basket collectors. Modern collectors had all but ignored the old firewood baskets until the gas crunch of the 1970s. Then, they began looking for them to again hold firewood—this time for woodburning stoves being installed. When fossil fuels became plentiful again, these baskets lost some of their appeal, but they're now being used as magazine racks.

There's only a hair's difference in basketry and wicker; in fact, in the early days, wicker was referred to as *basket furniture*. Today, many of the old firewood baskets cross the line and can be either basketry or wicker accessories.

Fish Traps

Basketmakers used whatever materials were available to make fish traps. In the southern part of the United States, a few basket fish traps can still be found. The old ones are made of oak and hickory splints. No doubt, river and swamp cane was used if basketmakers thought it would work. In the northern part of the country, roots seemed to be the favorite material.

The fish traps are similar to the eel traps, as they were designed along the same lines—to lure in fish but make it impossible for them to get out.

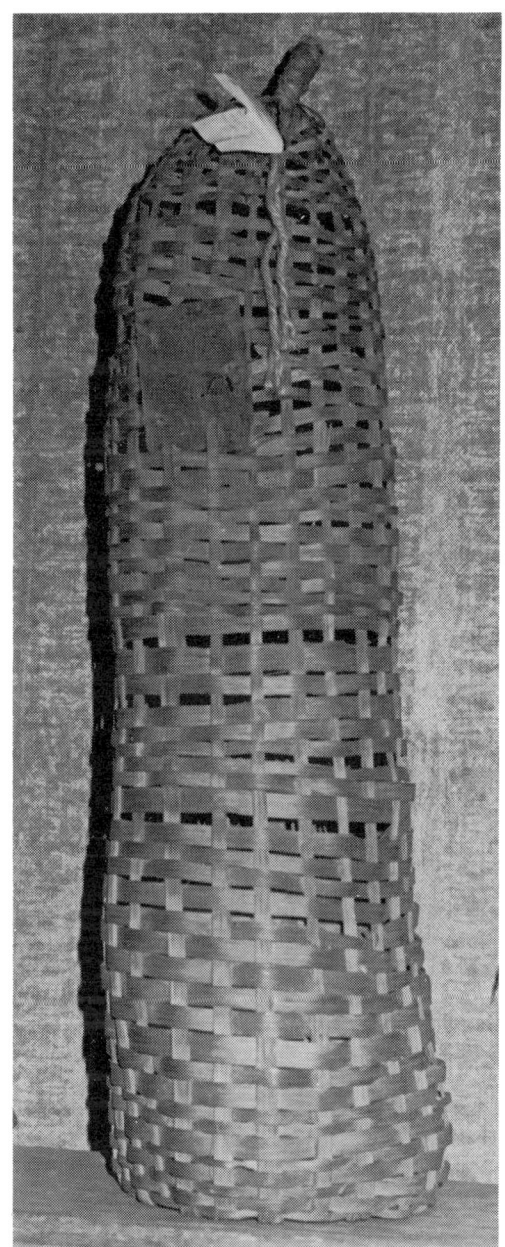

Fish trap. Private collection, NPA.

Five-Leaf Ivy

This name was used for Virginia Creeper in an effort to distinguish it from poison ivy. Virginia Creeper has a five-part leaf; poison ivy only has three. See Virginia Creeper.

Flag

Flag is the name given any of a number of plants that grow in marshes and bogs. It has sword-shaped leaves, and different species have different colored blossoms, including blue, purple, yellow, and white. See Rush and Cattails.

Flower-gathering basket.

Flower-Gathering Baskets

Flower-gathering baskets were usually round with slightly curved sides where the handle was attached. They came in several different sizes, but all were made to accommodate long stems. Most were made of either willow, reed, or rattan, while a few made of oak, hickory, and ash splints have been found.

Today, flower-gathering baskets are used more for magazine holders and fruit and vegetable displays than for gathering flowers.

Flower Pot Cuffs

Recently, there has been a revival of the use of greenery in the home. In the early part of this century, there was another revival. Then, as now, plants weren't left in plain flower pots, they were either put in fancy brass pots or the pots were covered in some other way. The earlier ones were covered by woven cuffs called *flower pot cuffs*.

Plain cuffs were made over cardboard or brown paper for a pleasing effect. Types listed in instruction books included braided grass in loops, cuffs trimmed with buttonholes, tied rush over matting, and knotted cuffs with buttonholed edges.

They were fragile, inexpensive things that were discarded when no longer needed, but this writer remembers them from childhood. A diligent search failed to uncover one for an illustration, but directions can be found in old basketry instruction books. A medium-sized pot required a circle or cuff 5–6 inches in diameter and 6–7 inches tall.

Forms or Molds for Baskets

In the Deep South, and in the mountains of Tennessee, Kentucky, and into Missouri, basket forms or molds were seldom used—basketmakers fashioned their baskets as they made them. In the northern states, however, especially New England, nearly everyone used forms for shaping their baskets.

A basketmaker might have dozens of forms or molds in assorted sizes. Basket forms were also used to make the now-famous Nantucket Lightship basket as well as the many ash and sweet-grass baskets made by New Englanders, including the Penobscots, Passamaquoddies, Micmacs, and Maliseets. The Shakers also used basket forms. The basket forms shown in the illustration belonged to the grandmother of a Penobscot lady who taught a basketry class on the reservation at Old Town, Maine.

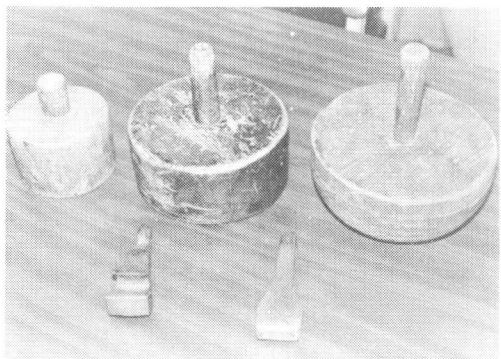

Three basket molds and two cutters for ash splints. Private collection, NPA.

Wicker fountain. 27" dia, 40" h. $3,500, Florida antique shop, summer 1986.

Fountain

The same over and under weaving that is used to make baskets is used to make wicker, but generally the wicker is a more refined version. The fountain (shown in the photograph) is thought to have been used in one of the luxury hotels during, or maybe shortly before, the Roaring Twenties, and is good example of refined over and under weaving. It is included here to show just how refined weaving can be.

There is a light in the center as well as a pump in the bottom that allowed the fountain to work. This formed a water base on which fresh flowers were placed.

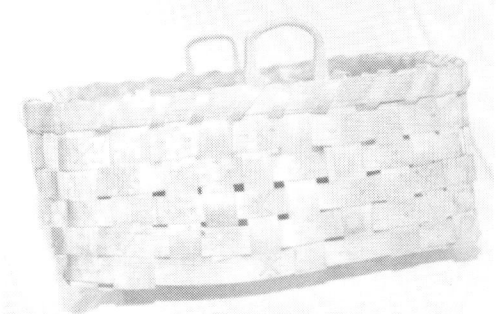

Freehand-decorated basket. 12" by 13" w, 4½" h. $48, Maine antique show, winter 1987.

Freehand-Design Painting

Potato or block painting was done by dipping a potato, turnip, or other block into dye, and then stamping the design on the weavers of the basket. Another type of decoration was the freehand-design painting. Several tribes of Indians, including the Algonkians, used this method of basket decoration in the early days. Instead of using the potato or block, they painted freehand dots and crosses on the basket. The designs may not be exactly alike from one weaver to the next, but they are similar.

Froe

The *froe* is more closely associated with shingle making than basketmaking, but many old basketmakers found it invaluable in making oak splints for baskets.

Fruit Gift Baskets

Shippers of gift fruits have long used baskets. The bright colors of the fruit against the white woven basket is very impressive. One firm—Harry and David of Medford, Oregon—realized that fact long ago and has been shipping gift fruit baskets since.

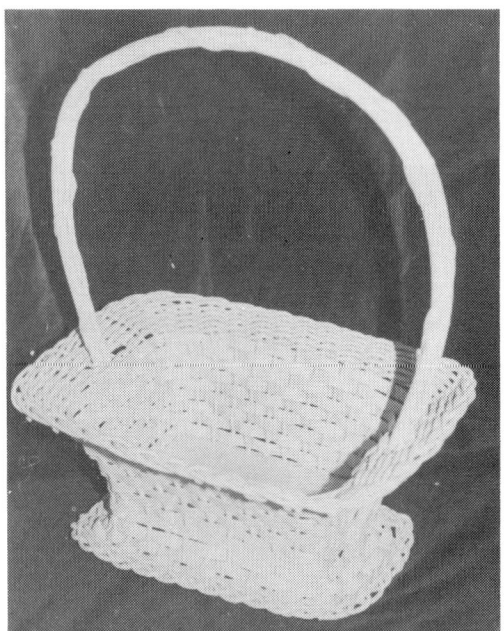

Fruit basket made in 1951. 13¼" l, 10" w, 16" o.h. $5, Maine Mall, fall 1986.

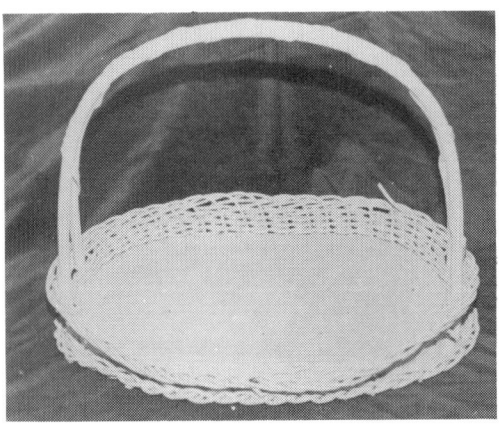

Shallow basket made in 1950. 10" w, 16" l, 11" o.h. $5, Vermont antique mall, winter 1986.

Harry and David trademark which appears on the two fruit baskets shown.

Now, the company's empty hand-woven baskets are turning up in flea markets and antique malls. They're easily identified as each is stamped on the bottom with the comapny name and the information that they were "handwoven and packed" by Harry and David. A check with the company revealed that it is probably the largest hand-woven basket factory in the country. No doubt, it uses a more or less assembly-line production basis. The baskets have wooden bottoms, which is essential for holding the weight of the fruit.

Fustic

A tropical tree of the mulberry family that is native to America. The wood chips of the fustic tree are used to make yellow dye, but if boiled too long, make a dark green dye.

Gift Basket

There is little difference between gift baskets and fruit gift baskets, except in the making. Fruit gift baskets are made by the company to hold fruits that will be shipped as a gift, while the gift basket will be carefully and lovingly made by one person to give to another. Of course, in earlier days the gift basket might come complete with a gift—maybe home grown fruit, vegetables, or even needlework—but always in the case of the gift basket, the basket itself was of utmost importance.

With the present revival of basket-making, the custom is being revived. Beautiful baskets are being made and given to friends and family. The new baskets may be filled with scented soaps, jams and jellies, homemade or bought. A basket, old or new, filled with a deck of playing cards, some paper back books, or maybe a few snacks makes a welcome gift for the shut-in.

Gizzard Basket

Another name for the buttocks basket. So-called because of the indented center rib. See Buttocks Basket.

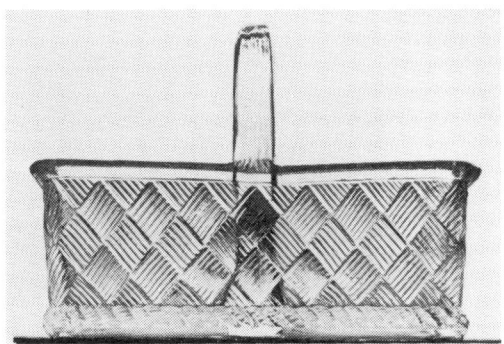

Glass basket. 2" w, 4" l, 5" o.h. $14, Tennessee antique shop, fall 1986.

Glass Baskets

Like Cinderella's slipper, both shoes and baskets were made of glass by glass companies, over a decade or so. Several types were made, but this one, which is one of the simpler examples, utilizes the woven basketry idea well.

Brass basket with white glass insert. 5" dia, 6" o.h. $35, Kansas antique shop, 1986.

Glass and Brass Basket

Decorative baskets were extremely popular a century or so ago, to fill the many whatnots in Victorian homes. The holly scene makes the one shown here especially attractive for use at Christmas. It could be used for nuts and candy as well.

Goldenback Fern

Goldenback is a fern that grows along the east coast and was often used as a substitute for maidenhair fern stems, which it closely resembles.

Golden Ragwort

The foliage of this wild plant of the thistle family is smooth and thin, and along with its stalk, is often slightly shaded to purple on the end. The rest of the long tough leaves and stalks are white, which gives the plant an unusual but lovely effect when used in coiled baskets. Another name for this plant is *Squaw grass.*

Gold Thread

Gold thread is an evergreen plant, *Coptis trifolia,* whose roots yield a clear, bright, lasting yellow. Dye from this plant was used in basketry, and its roots were used in medicine. See Yellow Dye.

Goose Basket

Long ago, a good homemaker was known by the number of feather beds in her home—with good down topping the list. To rise to the top of the social ladder in any community, she had to continue plucking geese and making feather beds.

A live goose whose feathers and down were plucked without the benefit of a sedative could get quite angry, and it's only recourse was pecking the picker. But housewives looking for both comfort and social status had to keep plucking, so for protection they bought goose baskets.

These baskets were made to fit over the head of the goose to prevent it from pecking. Some were made wider at the bottom to accommodate the goose's shoulders, while others were made about the same size from bottom to top. The baskets are long and narrow and the goose was put in the basket head first.

Straight-splint goose basket painted white. 10" dia, 22" h. $75, New Hampshire mall, fall 1986.

Miniature grapevine baskets made by the Cherokees. $8 each.

Some baskets were made to serve an additional purpose: Covers were made for the goose baskets which were used to store feathers and down until they could be used in mattresses and pillows.

Like many handmade items, goose baskets can be found in different sizes and shapes. Those from the South are mostly made of oak splints, while those from the Northeast are mostly made of ash splints.

Grapevine

Both wild and cultivated grape vines were used in basketry. They were often mixed with other vines, especially muscadine. Unlike so many other vines and ground runners, the roots of grape vines were also used, especially in weaving. New baskets coming in from the Philippines now have roots showing along the vines or ground runners, indicating they are probably grape or kudzu.

During the first half of this century, Boy Scouts were taught basketry as part of their woods and field training. It is safe to assume they used more grape vines in their baskets than any other kind, because they were easier to find.

Grass Twine

Hong Kong grass was also known by this name. See Hong Kong grass.

Green Dye

Very little green dye was used on baskets because it was so difficult to make. No green dye has been seen on old baskets from the South and Midwest; however, it was used sparingly in the Northeast and probably in Canada. It could be made, if one had the patience, by boiling together for quite some time, white cedar twigs and elm bark. The dye had to be set with copperas, and after all the time-consuming, tedious work, it seldom turned out to be a true green, but rather a yellow-green. Probably the only advantage of using green dye was that it seldom, if ever, faded.

Gullah Baskets

The *Gullah*, or Afro-American-made, baskets are famous all over the United States. These baskets have probably been made using the same method, for centuries. The Gullahs still make baskets exactly like their African ancestors.

Fortunately, their ancestors found almost the same type basket materials in America in the late 1600s. Although they lived in slavery on the plantations of South Carolina's Low Country, Afro-Americans continued to make baskets like their ancestors. The men made work baskets to be used on the plantations and in their own homes, and the women made pretty show baskets for use around the house, for gifts, or for selling.

Records from some of the old plantations show that as early as 1730, the black slaves were making and using *fanner* baskets for cleaning and winnowing rice. Fanning rice was a method similar to one used in West Africa. After the rice was harvested, it was put in a wooden mortar and pounded with a wooden pestle. This broke the hulls but didn't remove them from the rice. The rice then had to be taken from the mortar to a large, almost flat, coiled basket where it was thrown into the air (fanned) until the hulls or husks were removed from the grains.

Materials used in Gullah baskets.

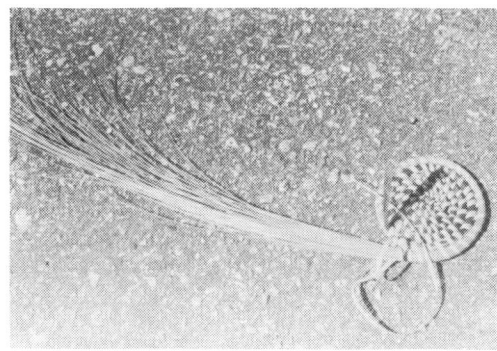

The grass is coiled, and then sewn together with palmetto strips.

The Gullah baskets on the left are old; those on the right are new. Prices range from $10 to $25 each.

Roadside stand showing variety of Gullah baskets.

Seldom are the four materials, sea grass—often called sea straw by the workers—bull rush, pine needles, and palmetto, used in any one basket, but all four of the materials are used in Gullah basketry. A tougher rush or grass called *rushel* is now being used in some of their baskets. Pine needles are added more for color than as a material.

Display of baskets. Prices on the new baskets range from $20 to $55 each.

This craft has been handed down from mother to daughter and father to son for generations. Although few work baskets are made now, both boys and girls are taught to make them. During the last half century, this sort of basketmaking has developed into a rather lucrative business. Basketmakers now have stands along the highways that afford them a chance to show and sell their baskets while allowing them to take care of their homes and children. The stands of over 60 families are located on U.S. Highway 60, in the community of Mt. Pleasant, just outside of Charleston, South Carolina.

Incidentally, Gullah is a language of more than one race of people, but it has been used so long in connection with Low Country baskets that they are best known as Gullah baskets.

Gullah Show Baskets

So-called show baskets were and still are made of sea grass sewn together with split palmetto (palm) leaves. The use of these two materials makes the baskets light and colorful. Show baskets were first made around 1900. When the coastal highway was paved outside Charleston in the 1920s, women there began selling their baskets in stands outside their homes. Today, there are over 60 family-operated stands on the four-mile stretch of U.S. Highway 17.

Gullah Work Baskets

Men always made the work baskets because they had to be tough enough to be used on the farms. To give them great strength, they were made of bull rushes sewn together with thin white oak splints or split palmetto butts. Now there is little to no demand for work baskets, but the men occasionally make the large baskets.

Display of large Gullah-made baskets. New.

Hair was stuffed through the hole in the top of a hair receiver, and it was opened to take it out. 4" dia, 6" h. $25, Maine antique show, 1987.

Hair Receivers (Baskets)

Hair receivers were made in silver, hand-painted china, glass, celluloid, and basketry. Before the Flapper era, most women wore their hair long. Often they would save the hair left in their combs to make "rats," paddings over which the hair could be combed to give it a "full" effect, similar to the Gibson Girl look. The hair receiver was used to store the hair until enough was collected to make a rat.

Hana-Kago

The Japanese name for baskets made exclusively for flower arranging is *hana-kago*. Long known as leaders in flower arranging, the Japanese made their own baskets, perhaps with the idea that they could be made to complement each other. These baskets were used for *ikebana* (fresh flowers) and for *zokwa*, to decorate with artificial flowers. It's possible some of the old hana-kago are now finding their way into the states since there is so much travel between the two countries.

Ash-splint and sweet-grass handkerchief box. 7¼" square, 2¼" h. $55, Rhode Island antique shop, fall 1986.

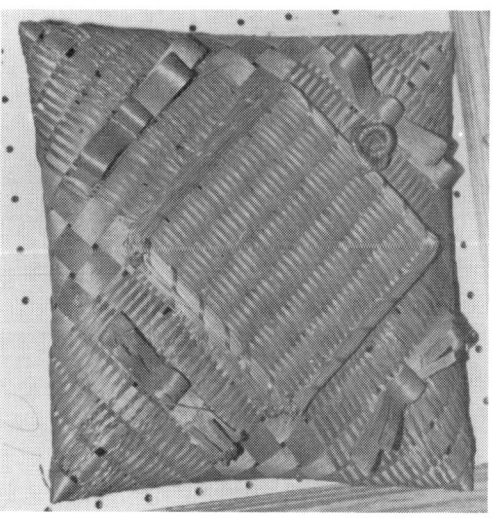

Ash-splint and sweet-grass handkerchief box, Penobscot Museum, NPA.

Handkerchief Boxes

Basket handkerchief boxes are believed to have been strictly tourist-trade items. While other types may have been made, in the northeast part of the United States, square handkerchief baskets with a center

Ash-splint and sweet-grass handkerchief box, Unity College collection, NPA.

Bushel basket of oak splints with good handles.

Ash-splint basket with a handle that is too low.

opening were the most popular. Also, ash-splint and sweet-grass handkerchief boxes were made—plain with solid tops that swung open.

Making basketry items for the tourist-trade could be quite lucrative. The Abenakis, a Canadian tribe, spends summers in the states making basketry items to be sold at large resorts. One such basketmaker reported an income of over $4,000 back in 1910. Of course, she worked all during the winter, and then in summer she hired other basketmakers to help her fill orders and keep her stand stocked.

Some handkerchief boxes had round lift tops and others had square ones, but all were made of a combination of paper-thin ash splints and sweet grass. Some had narrow dyed splints; others had decorations of bows and curlicues made of thin splints.

In those days, a handkerchief was a very necessary part of one's outfit. Handkerchiefs were always fancy, usually with delicate embroidery or a lace border.

Handles for Baskets

The old basketmakers who also carved designs and whittled toys often made exquisite designs on basket handles. But whether it was fancy or not, the emphasis was always on a strong, sturdy handle—one that was strong enough to carry the weight of the basket and its contents.

Although it was important to have a strong handle, basketmakers emphasized that the handle also had to be graceful and in proportion with the basket.

Ash-splint basket with a beautifully proportioned handle.

The type of handle varied with the whims and skills of the maker. Some made rope handles while others used the braided, wrapped, or looped handles. Then there were those who never varied their basketmaking methods or styles; they continued to make good, solid splint handles.

Coushatta-made pine needle wall hanging. 7" h, 8" w. $15, Coushatta reservation, spring 1986.

Penobscot-made ash-splint and sweet-grass wall hanging, Unity College collection, NPA.

Hanging Ornamental Baskets

Any basketmaker working with long pine needles is apt to try different ways of coiling the needles into something interesting and decorative. This is especially true of the Coushatta Indians of Louisiana who have a history of making unusual pine needle basketry items. One unusual item is a wall hanging in the shape of a cup and saucer. In the Northeast, the Indians made another type of wall hanging—a circle with a tall, staggered top.

Derby powder-puff box, Unity College collection, NPA.

Sailor hat powder-puff box. 6½" dia, 3" h. $48, Maryland antique shop, fall 1986.

Hats

Straw hats are believed to have come in vogue around summer theatres. Regardless of where it started, the craze soon spread across the country. Early in the twentieth century, few men dared to go out in the summer without wearing a Panama straw hat.

The flat-topped style straw hat became known as a *skimmer* when worn by the men, and a *sailor* when worn by a women. In resort areas, men wore white pants, blue blazers, and straw hats, while the ladies wore white embroidered dresses and sailor straw hats.

Basketmakers in those areas took notice and designed small souvenir-type basketry hats. All were made of sweet grass and paper-thin splints of ash. The ladies hats were made in two pieces; when the tops are removed, there is a place to store her powder puff.

Hazelwood

The hazel tree has served many purposes: It grows delicious hazel nuts, or filberts; was used in wooden-boat building; and the wood is so light and flexible, it's perfect for basketmaking. All hazel wood is light; in fact, it's so light, the Hupa Indians used it to make most of their burden baskets. The branches or shoots could be used for both the spokes and weavers.

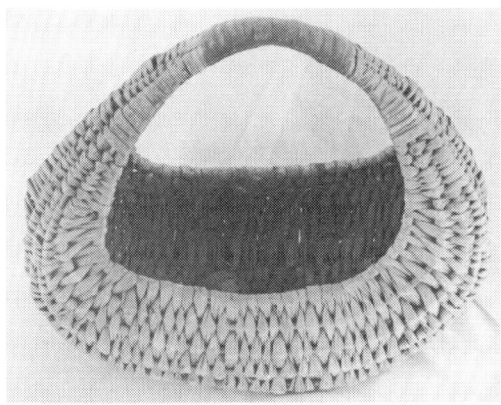

Hen basket. 8" w, 13" l, 13" o.h. $35, Maine auction, fall 1986.

Hen Baskets

Before the advent of electricity and incubators, it was the custom to allow a hen to lay a nest full of eggs and then "set" on her eggs until her chicks hatched. Or, if a hen indicated she was in a "setting or nesting" mood, she would be given a nest full of eggs. Some hens would raise one brood of chicks and almost immediately start with another. In some areas, these were known as good *broody hens.*

Since not all hens were good broody hens, one family might not be able to raise enough chicks for the next year. Often, though, a neighbor might loan a good brooding hen to others in the community who were not as fortunate.

Hen baskets were made to transport the hens back and forth. The same baskets could be used to transport extra hens to the general store to be sold or traded for other things. The baskets are believed to be of English origin.

Hemlock

Hemlock trees are found from Nova Scotia to Alabama. Its wood has been used widely and in many different ways by basketmakers, since it adjusts easily to fit the needs of the makers. For basketmakers, the most important part of the tree is the roots which usually are split before using.

Wide split-cane hanging basket with hexagon weave, late. 11" h, 10½" × 7½" opening. $15, Alabama antique shop.

Hexagon-weave basket. 18" dia, 14" h. $40, Maine antique show, fall 1986.

Hexagon Weave

Most basketmakers, regardless of location, used the hexagon or honeycomb weave. This weave may have originated with cheese baskets, most of which were made using the hexagon weave, but its use is not restricted to cheese baskets. You'll find many different types of baskets with a hexagon weave.

Hickey-made willow basket with handles on either side. Private collection, NPA.

Hickey Baskets

The first name of this old basketmaker is unknown. Earlier in this century, people would seek out a man named *Hickey* who came each spring with a load of beautiful, well-made willow baskets. If an individual didn't have the money to purchase one of Mr. Hickey's baskets, he would trade them for chickens, or eggs, or another commodity.

The way the handle is attached is a trademark of Hickey baskets. Private collection, NPA.

Well-made hickory-splint basket. 19" dia, 13" h. $110, Maine auction, fall 1986.

Hickory Splint

The hickory tree, a member of the walnut family, is one of America's toughest trees. It has been used to make cane chairs—chairs destined for rough and tough service, usually in families with many children.

Hickory splints have never been as popular as oak splints for making spokes and weavers. They were, however, very popular for making basket handles because they were tough and durable.

Hines, Regina

Contemporary Georgia basketmaker who has perfected the art of *kudzu vine* basketmaking. Now teaches her craft in area colleges.

Holygrass

Little information can be found on this species of grass, indicating the name is one used by local basketmakers. It reportedly grows only in the northern part of the United States. Its long, sweet-smelling leaves are twisted and braided to make basket weavers. It is also wrapped for use in coiled baskets.

Honeycomb Weave

Another name for hexagon weave. See Hexagon Weave.

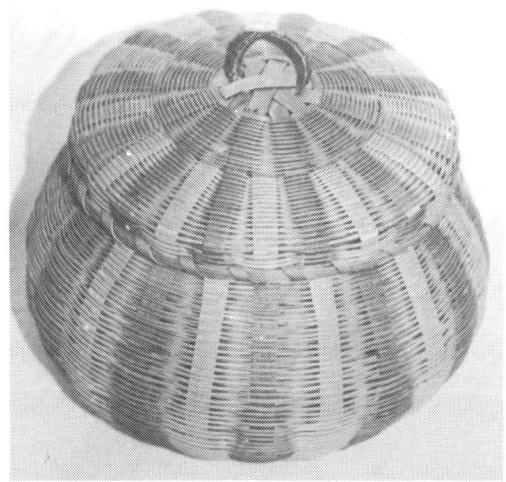

Covered splint and honeysuckle basket, Unity College collection, NPA.

Honeysuckle Vine

Many vines can be used to make baskets, but probably none are more widely used than honeysuckle. Its popularity can be attributed to the fact that honeysuckle grows wild all over the country. The Cherokees used vines more often than anyone else, with the possible exception of mountain basketmakers.

Care must be taken when gathering this vine. Cherokees insist that the honeysuckle, or any other vine used in basketry, be gathered in the fall. Only the past year's growth should be taken. Vines that have been allowed to grow for several years will have small branches growing on them, and when removed, will leave rough places that detract from the smoothness of the vine. Vines may be used alone or combined with splints to make baskets. Any of the vines can be dyed.

Lift-top box made of Hong Kong grass and ash splints, has a sweet-grass border. 4½" square, 2½" h. $25, New England antique shop, fall 1986.

Yarn basket of Hong Kong grass and ash splints. 7" dia, 11" h. $47.50, Maine antique shop, fall 1986.

Hong Kong Grass

Half a century or so ago, the Chinese devised a method of twisting sea grass while it was held under water. This technique resulted in a product closely resembling small rope.

Urn-shaped waste basket, ash splint and Hong Kong grass with sweet-grass border. 8½" dia 11½" h. $46, New England antique show, fall 1986.

Hong Kong grass was imported for use in both basketmaking and chair caning. It was very popular because it was handmade and fit right into the scheme of handmade baskets. It was also very inexpensive.

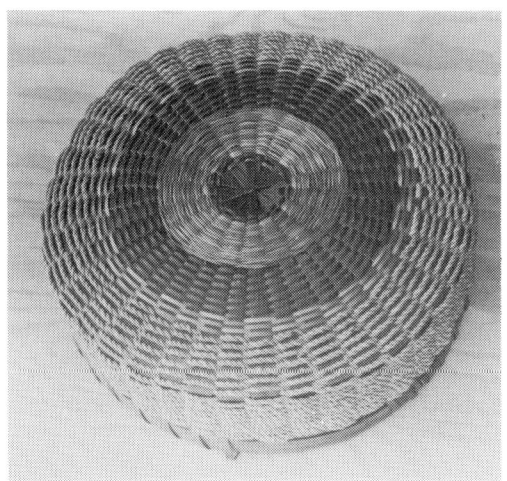

Basket cover of Hong Kong grass, and ash splints, with a center of sweet grass. Cover only 9½" dia, 2½" h. $5, Maine antique shop.

Hopi wickerwork peach basket. 10½" dia, 9½" h. $150, Maine auction, winter 1986.

Knowledge of basketry and basketry materials is essential, today, to distinguish between the braided and twisted sweet grass used by the Indians of the Northeast, and imported Hong Kong grass. These two types of grasses were often combined in one basket.

It was much easier to use Hong Kong grass as it didn't have to be gathered and dyed. It could be bought in red, green, blue, brown, orange, and natural. It sold in three- and four-pound *hanks*, with each hank consisting of approximately 300 feet of twisted sweet grass.

The natural color was a beautiful beige or tan that blended in perfectly with paper-thin ash splints. It was used in large amounts when making tourist trade items. Hong Kong grass was also called *grass twine*.

Hopi Indians

Today, about three fourths of the 10,000 members of the Hopi tribe live on the 641,000-acre Hopi reservation in Arizona. The name *Hopi* is derived from the Shoshone language and means "peaceful ones." They call themselves Moqui, and are basically farmers.

Peaches are one of the better Hopi crops, and apparently always have been. Government reports from the 1880s on Indian affairs often have pictures of peach baskets, usually identified as Hopi peach baskets. Many tribes raised peaches, but none with the prestige and flair of the Hopi, whose trees were originally sent to them by Queen Isabella of Spain.

The Hopi made very fine peach baskets, but their basketry extended beyond that. They were, and still are well known for their excellent basketry of all types. Like their Indian neighbors in the Southwest, the Hopi made coiled and wickerwork trays and baskets of rabbit brush, sumac, wild currant bush, and yucca. And like their basketmaking neighbors, they wove designs in their baskets—designs representing their dreams, surroundings, and religion.

Horse-Feeding Basket

Horse-feeding baskets like the one shown here were made by a number of different Indian tribes. They were filled with grain and fastened to the horse's bridle so he could eat while away from home.

Ash-splint horse-feeding basket made by the Maliseet Indians. 12" dia, 13" h. $125, Maine antique show, winter 1986.

Hupa Baby Basket

From the instant a Hupa Indian baby was born, it was placed in an open-weave basket where it would remain for the next ten days. Later, the child would have a standing type cradle or carrier that was also carried on the mother's back.

Unlike the later Indian baby carriers, the shallow, round, open-weave carriers are believed to have been used by the Hupa Indians. Baskets were so important to the Hupa, they could actually say they began life in a basket. The Hupa believed that placing a newborn infant in a basket, along with subjecting it to various treatments, would ward off evil, and the infant's good health would be assured.

It was customary for the grandmother to make both the open weave baby basket and the cradle the mother would use later. Both were made of peeled shoots of the hazelnut tree. The baby basket was called a *kaitel*.

Iizuka Hosia

Around the turn of the century, Iizuka was one of the best known of the Tokyo basketmakers.

Indian Currant

This plant is also called coralberry, coral bush, and buckbush, (the latter name was given to it by mountain basketmakers who probably weren't aware of other names).

Indian currant is a shrub of the honeysuckle family used as a basketry material in the southern and eastern states. Once the vines have been cleaned and peeled, it's difficult to distinguish between Indian currant and honeysuckle. It's not unusual for basketmakers to mix several types of vines in one basket.

Indigo

Indigo is a plant used to make blue dyes for either fabric or basket materials. The most commonly cultivated species of this plant in America, is *indigofera tinctoria*. It's a shrub-type plant that grows to heights of three and four feet.

Oldtimers kept a dye pot, usually indigo, ready at all times. It was used to dye wool for both clothing and coverlets. In the South and Midwest, indigo was used more sparingly on baskets, but in the Northeast it was used extensively on both wool yarns and basket materials.

The shades of blue will vary, as the color depends on the strength of dye used when the material was dyed. Sometimes the dye was first used on wools or splints, and then the leftovers were used on basket materials.

This dye was easy to prepare and easy to apply. In fact, it was very easy to apply using the Indian method of swabbing one side of the ash splint with a piece of fabric or the soft skin of an animal. The paper-thin ash splints used by most New England Indians were so thin, the dye soaked right through it.

Shopping bag made of Hong Kong grass and dark blue ash splints. 6" w, 13½" l, 9½" h. $40, Massachusetts antique shop, fall 1986.

Ash-splint and sweet-grass jewelry box. 5" dia, 4" o.h. $38, Maine antique show, 1987.

Jewelry basket attributed to Shakers. Private collection, NPA.

Jewelry Basket

The small jewelry and sewing baskets were interchangeable, but the ones most readily acceptable for jewelry were small and round with three feet. The square and oblong style that opened on top were also used.

Finely coiled tray could have been made by the Jicarillas. Lightner Museum, NPA.

Jicarilla Indians

The Jicarillas were part of the Apache tribe that lived in northern New Mexico. The Apaches were somewhat nomadic, probably because they were constantly searching for water and less arid lands. The Jicarillas lived in teepees in open country, but built brush shelters when in the mountains. They practiced some agriculture, but depended mostly on wild plants, seeds, and game. Unlike so many of the other Indians, they did not become skilled in weaving, nor did they make much pottery, but they did make fine baskets.

Many of their early baskets had little or no decoration. When they began to sell baskets to the white collectors, they added designs. Their work was exquisite and it was said that as many as 100,000 stitches might be used in one large tray. The work was so intricate it might take a year to complete a large tray.

Kaitel

The Indian name for the Hupa baby basket. See Hupa Baby Basket.

Kakisookbe

Kakisookbe is the old term the Penobscots used for ash splints. It meant the splints were very flexible and would not break easily, a necessary feature when making fancy designs on baskets. See Wicopy.

Kettle Baskets

No explanation has been found for making baskets in the shape of old iron kettles. Somebody probably decided to copy the shape and others followed suit.

Large kettle basket made of thicker ash splints. Different swing handle. Unity College collection, NPA.

Small kettle basket made of ash splints and sweet grass. Unity College collection, NPA.

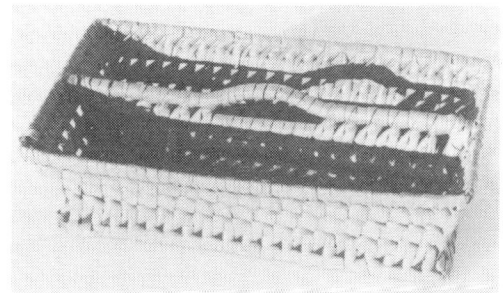

Late basketry knife box. 6" w, 11" l, 2¾" h. $20, Maine antique show, 1987.

Knife Box, Basketry

The most desirable knife boxes are, of course, the early upright ones with Sheraton or other early cabinetmakers' influence. The average knife box is wooden with a handle in the center. These basketry knife boxes were used on the family eating tables, and often held all the flatware. Some preferred to use them in conjunction with the wooden knife boxes.

Knotted Carrying Baskets

It's not clear who made the first netted carrying baskets. The Indians made them using a variety of fibers, and the white sailors are known to have knotted everything from baskets to canopies for the bed.

Knotted carrying baskets are no longer needed, but old sailors continue to knot small souvenir-type baskets.

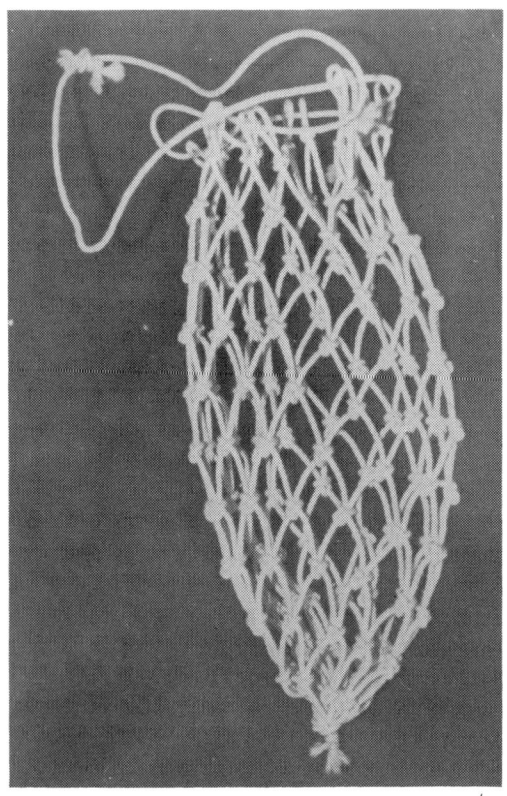

New, small knotted carrying basket. 8" l. $3, Massachusetts antique shop, 1987.

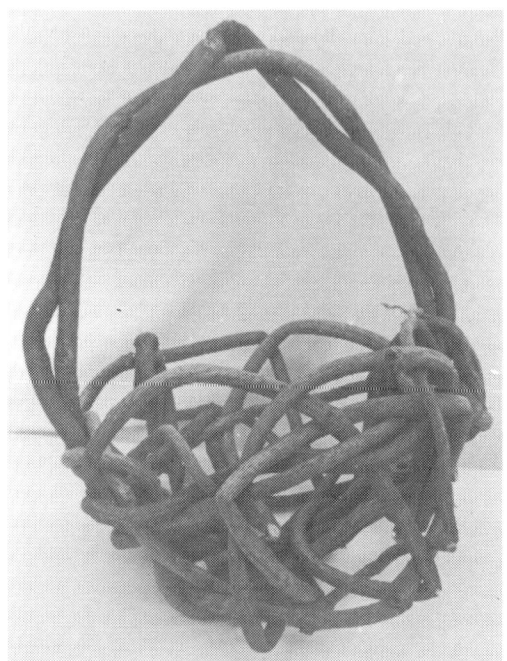

Free-form kudzu basket. 11" dia, 16" o.h. $25, Georgia maker, 1986.

Koasati Indians

Another name for the Louisiana Coushattas. See Coushatta.

Kudzu Vine

Oriental *kudzu* was imported into the southern states for two reasons—to help stop soil erosion and feed livestock. It has served its purpose well in both areas. The fast-growing vine has been checked and measured to determine its overnight growth. Experts agree it will grow as much as 18 inches overnight. Even though this vine makes good cattle feed, it grows so quickly, the cattle can't keep it under control.

Traditional basket made of split kudzu vine. 9½" w, 11" l, 15" o.h. $25, Georgia maker, 1986.

During the summer, the landscape in parts of the South is often a sea of green leaves as kudzu vines spread over the trees, utility poles, and anything else in its path. People who dislike kudzu, and there are plenty of them, have been unable to eradicate it. Therefore, there was rejoicing in Georgia when one of their own, Regina Hines, began making baskets using kudzu vines. At first she made traditional baskets, but then she noticed that the vines grew in beautiful—if sometimes grotesque—shapes, so she began making free-form baskets.

The vines are gathered in early spring or late fall while they are still reasonably green. Completely dried or dead vines are too brittle and will break as one works with them. Small vines can be used in the traditional baskets, or the large ones can be split. The bark, or outside, is left on the vines to give them an instant antique appearance. Hines has built a thriving basket business in Georgia; in fact, kudzu baskets became so popular, she now teaches a class at the local college.

La Passiance

La Passiance are the roots of the dock plant, any of several course weeds of the buckwheat family, used by the Chitimacha Indians to obtain the rich, bright red used in their cane baskets.

Lazy Squaw Weave

This was one of the first weaves described in the Navajo basket-weaving book published in 1903. The explanation was very interesting because it explained why the weaver would leave large spaces in the weave. In those days, the reed or rod was called a *bam*. It was said that if the squaw was lazy when making a basket, she would wrap the bam, or reed, two to four times before making the much harder stitch that was necessary to hold the reeds or bams together in the coiling of the foundation. The other squaws would criticize her and call her a lazy squaw; hence, the name for that stitch. This stitch does leave open spaces in an otherwise closely coiled basket.

The inside of a large ash-splint lid.

Lids and Covers

The majority of the old splint baskets didn't have lids or covers in the beginning, and some of those that did have been lost through the years. On the other hand, Indian-made baskets, especially the fancy kind made in the Northeast, all seem to have had lids and covers. For most work and burden baskets, they really weren't necessary, but for the fancy ones, they were necessary and they made the baskets much prettier.

Making tops that would fit the baskets and boxes required more than ordinary skill. Actually, skill and experience, and maybe a little wizardry were required to make lids for the small pine needle baskets—lids that must fit easily, yet firmly, in the inside of the small opening.

Lids were, and still are, made in several different shapes. The Coushatta Indians make lids with collars for their pine needle baskets. A *collared* lid is made with an inside collar that fits the lid perfectly inside the basket, regardless of its size or shape. The northeastern Indians also used collared lids, but many were flat, or they were lids with turned-down sides. Domed lids were made for the larger baskets.

Lord, Albra

Lord was a Lovell, Maine basketmaker who made excellent baskets during the late 1800s and early 1900s. His baskets, especially the swing-handle ones, are very sought after by Mainers. Today, authentic Lord baskets bring exhorbitant prices. His baskets are round with weavers that widen as they reach the top. The swing handles are fastened with copper rivets.

Lumbee Indians

Mystery surrounds the Lumbees. From the mid 1800s to the mid 1900s they were called Croatans. Speculation links them to the Lost Colony—the white settlers who vanished centuries ago—but no proof has been found to substantiate the theory. Then, there are those who believe the settlers intermarried with the Hatteras Indians and later migrated to the banks of the Lumber River in North Carolina. Due to their close association with white settlers, and their location in the Great Smoky Mountain area, the Lumbee Indians have always made oak-splint baskets as well as vine baskets.

Same type splint basket as made by a Lumbee. Private collection, NPA.

Mahogany Roots

Navajo Indians used the roots of the mahogany tree to make dye for the sumac they used to make baskets. Lumber from the trees might have been important to furniture makers, but the Indians of the Southwest were only interested in the roots to make a reddish brown dye. The older Navajo women referred to it as "mountain mahogany."

Maidenhair Fern Stems

There are approximately 200 species of maidenhair fern. Only one, though, grows heartily in the north, American maidenhair. It is safe to assume that American maidenhair, or five-finger fern (pedatum), was the type of maidenhair fern used in the baskets made in America. Indian basketmakers used the stems more in their basketry than the whites. Generally, the fern stems were combined with spruce roots to make tightly woven or twined baskets.

Magazine Racks

Magazine racks were not made in a variety of styles until after the turn of the century. Before the twentieth century, there weren't many magazines being published. Those magazines that were published weren't receiving much distribution.

Woven-splint magazine rack. 13" w, 18" l, 10" h. $25, Vermont flea market, 1986.

Thus, there wasn't a big demand for magazine racks, and basketmakers felt no compulsion to make them. They knew other baskets would sell, so why bother to make a new item with a questionable future? With the introduction of gas and steam heat, the need for the old woven firewood baskets decreased, and owners simply converted them to magazine racks. Surprisingly, no instructions for magazine racks were found in the old basketry books.

Old Makah basket of cedar roots twined with grass. 3" dia 1¾" h, $105, New Hampshire mall, fall 1986.

Makah Indians

The Makahs have long been considered one of the more daring of the tribes living in the Northwest. Long before the arrival of the white man, they would go completely out of sight of land to search for whales. Since the whales were much larger than the boats, they would tow in the dead whale behind the little boat. They were so skilled in ocean travel, they could go out of sight of land and return, guided only by atmospheric conditions and the direction of the waves.

As in most Indian tribes, the women were the basketmakers, and shortly before the turn of the present century, they began making inexpensive, tourist-type baskets. They might have been inexpensive then, but they are very expensive now.

Being whaler families, they used that theme in many of their baskets. Their work is similar to other tribes in that area, especially the Nootka of British Columbia.

Most Makah baskets were made of cedar roots twined with bear grass, and they usually begin with a checkerwork bottom. The majority of the Makah baskets found today are twines, but they did, at an earlier time, make coiled baskets. Most of their baskets are lidded and are small, usually under eight inches.

Maliseet Indians

There are only about 2500 Maliseets living in Maine at the present time, but several centuries ago they were a powerful tribe, one to be reckoned with. They were semi-agricultural—grew some corn, squash, and probably a few other things—but depended mainly on hunting and fishing for their food. Like so many other tribes of that era, they usually moved on regular basis as they looked for better hunting and fishing grounds. Normally, the Maliseets resided near large bodies of water, as they were a seafaring people, and have been described as bold sailors who hunted seal, porpoise, and whale.

This ash-splint basket was often called a carrying basket. 10" dia, 12" h. $48, Vermont flea market, 1986.

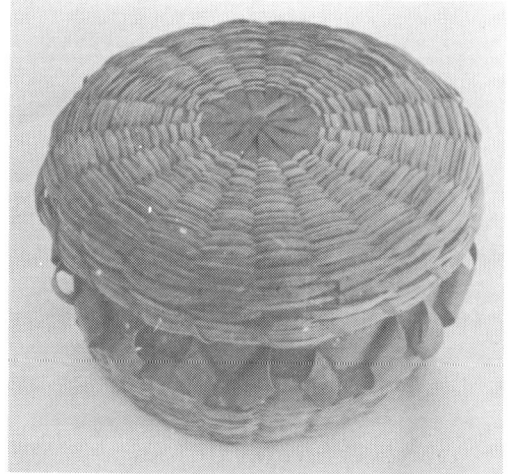

Ash-splint and sweet-grass covered basket. 4" dia, 2½" h. $18, New Hampshire mall, fall 1986.

For some reason, this type basket, made of Hong Kong and sweet grass with ash splints, was called an arm basket, in Canada, 10" dia, 6" h, $43, Maine antique show, 1986.

Ash-splint basket typical of those made by the Maliseets. Unity College collection, NPA.

They were so closely associated with other Maine tribes (the Penobscots, Passamaquoddies, and Micmacs), and their work was so similar, it's difficult today for the average collector to differentiate between the baskets made by each tribe. Not only were the same basket materials available to all of them, they were also vying for the same tourist trade. Although they still won't admit it, they are believed to have "borrowed" ideas from one another and from the white basketmakers.

Older baskets, those 150 to 200 years old, are not easy to find. For that reason, it's almost impossible to compare the earlier work of these tribes with their later basketry—the items made for the tourist trade. However, they did excellent work and apparently made thousands of baskets during their heyday.

Mallet

This tool is used like a hammer and is roughly the length of an ax. The handle is shaped to fit the hand while the eight- to ten-inch hammer-type head is left on the other end. The head is used to pound a wedge into oak trees to split them. The mallet is sometimes used to beat the ash so it will separate into the annual growth splints.

Oak-splint market basket. 13" w, 17" l, 16" o.h. $225, Kentucky antique shop, 1986.

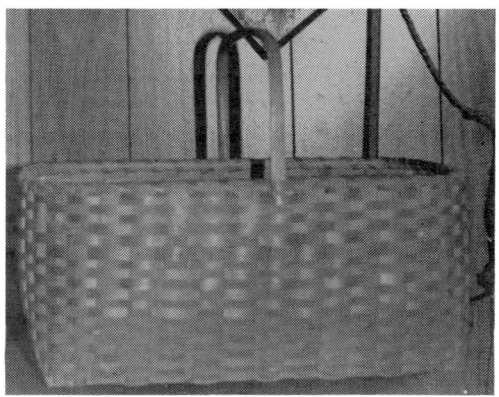

Ash-splint market basket. 12" w, 14" l, 15" o.h. $65, Maine auction, fall 1986.

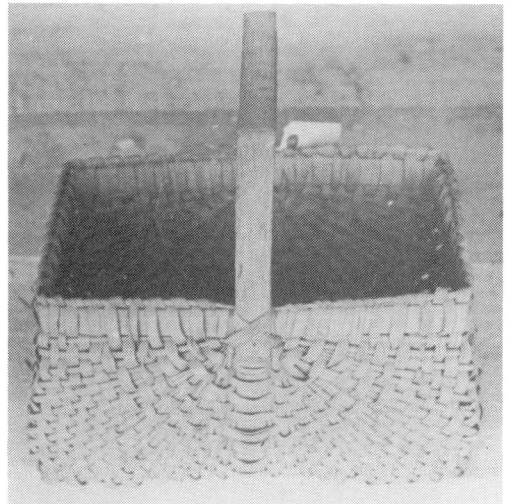

Oak-splint market basket from the mountain areas. 10" w, 12" l, 14" o.h. $350, Tennessee antique shop, 1986.

Market Baskets

It has been said that when the paper bag, the poke, and the cardboard carton replaced the handmade basket, we all became a little poorer.

At one time, the ladies living in cities, towns, and villages across the country took their beautiful handmade baskets over their arms each morning and sallied forth to buy food for the day. There was no way to preserve food other than canning or smoking; therefore, they chose the simpler and better way of buying fresh foods daily.

Larger-than-usual market basket. Private collection, NPA.

Indian-made ash-splint market basket, reinforced rim. 12" w, 14" l, 15" o.h. $75, Maine auction, fall 1986.

Factory-made market basket, materials unknown. 12" w, 20" l, 14" o.h. $45, Maine estate sale, summer 1986.

It is not unusual, now, to find old pictures showing a housewife going from one place to another with her market basket over her arm. There were no super markets and few general stores in those days. Instead, she shopped with independent merchants like the vegetable vendors, butchers, and those selling fresh fruits.

The style, shape, and design of the market basket might differ from one area to another depending on the skills of the basketmaker and the preference of the housewife. Location also had a bearing on style and shape. Most were open, but occasionally covered ones can be found. It was easier for the shopper to drop her purchases in an open basket, and also, they would hold more than the closed baskets.

Some market baskets were made stronger than ordinary baskets—food could be heavy to carry.

The market basket was also used for other shopping trips; there were no large shopping bags made of paper in the dry goods stores in those days. It was much easier to use the market basket or a smaller shopping basket than try to keep up with numerous loose packages.

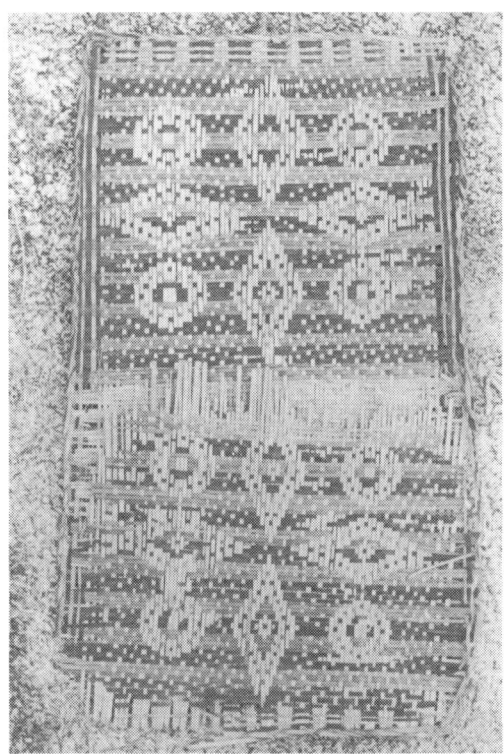

Old Chitimacha cane mat with worn edges and center. Private collection, NPA.

Mats

Basketmakers skilled in basketry made other things using the basketry techniques of weaving, coiling, and twining. After the twisting, turning, and shaping of baskets, it must have been easy to make flat items like mats. Mats were necessary and were made by most of the Indians, especially those east of the Plains. Mats served a dual role— they could be used as decorative wall hangings, or they could be used as floor mats for the family to sit on when eating or visiting.

Usually made of river or swamp cane, these mats were dyed the same as other basketry materials. Few are made today except those made to be sold in arts and crafts outlets.

Maul

Maul is another name for mallet. See Mallet.

May Baskets

Until recently, it was customary for children and some adults to take small baskets of flowers to the sick and the shut-ins, or as an expression of appreciation to someone who had been kind to them.

It's believed the custom was a variation of the old English custom of "Going a-Maying." It was customary during the sixteenth and seventeenth centuries for the middle and lower classes to go out early in the morning on the first day of May, to gather flowers and hawthorn branches. The hawthorn blossom was named *May*, which accounts for the term "bringing home the May." Early in the morning they would go merrily into the woods and fields, accompanied by the music of a horn, and gather flowers and greenery. Around sunrise they would have enough to decorate all the doors and houses in the village, and would return to the village to begin that task.

In earlier times, kings and queens attended these festivities, which probably accounted for their popularity then. May Day festivities became so famous, they were celebrated throughout the British Empire.

Miccosukee Indians

The Miccosukees acknowledge that their origin has been lost and now only lives in legends, but they're proud of being part of the Creek confederacy—a loosely organized group of Indians living along the rivers and creeks of Alabama, Georgia, and the Carolinas. The Miccosukees were niether nomadic nor war-like. They preferred living, farming, hunting, and fishing in the same area.

First few rows of a coiled basket on patchwork background.

Materials used in making Miccosukee baskets with an almost-finished basket.

Sweet-grass basket with doll head finial. $90, Miccosukee reservation, spring 1986. New.

Pine needle basket with colorful design, new. $130, Miccosukee reservation, spring 1986.

Early in the eighteenth century, a group known as the Mikasukis settled near what is now Tallahassee, Florida. The name soon took on the phonetic sound, *Miccosukee,* the name they are known by today. When the Miccosukee were to be sent to Oklahoma with other Indians, many of them hid in the Everglades and remained there in hiding until around 1870 when they began trading furs, plumes, and hides for supplies. The government soon passed laws prohibiting the sale of egret plumes and alligator hides, so they returned to their *chickees* in the Everglades.

A chickee is a house of sorts, or dwelling, designed and built by the Miccosukee in the Everglades, using the available materials and built to suit the hot, humid weather. A typical chickee is approximately 16 feet long by 9 feet wide, and is built on a platform about 3 feet off the ground. The purpose of elevating the homes is, of course to protect the people from floods, but also to protect them from snakes and other creatures of the Everglades. Cypress poles are used to support the roof, and smaller cypress poles are used to hold the cabbage palm or palmetto fronds that are used to cover the roof.

Although it upset the ecology of the Everglades, somewhat, building the Tamiami Trail that connects Miami with the west coast of Florida was a blessing for the Miccosukee. It has brought hundreds of tourists past their doors—tourists who stop to buy the beautiful patchwork for which they are justly famous, as well as their paintings, dolls, beadwork, wood carvings, and pine needle baskets.

Through the years, the Miccosukees have used many basket materials indigenous to the area, such as cane, cabbage palm stalks, grasses, fronds, strips of bark, and pine needles. But in recent years, most of their basketmaking for the tourist trade has been pine needles. They use the coil technique, but with a difference—the base of the basket is made with a circle of strong cardboard covered on both sides with palmetto fiber. The coiling starts on the edge of the circle.

Another difference in their baskets is that instead of using raffia, as do other basketmakers when working with pine needles, they use brilliantly colored thread that's been pulled through beeswax to strengthen it. Like the raffia, the thread is used to make designs.

Micmac Indians

The first meeting between the Micmac Indians in Maine and the white settlers occurred on the coast near Cape Neddick in 1602. At that time, they called themselves Ul'noo or *the people.* The corruption began with the term *nikmag* which meant kin-friend, an indication of their relationship with the whites. The nikmag name tag stuck and eventually became Micmac, despite the fact the French originally called them Souriquois, and the English referred to them as Tarentines.

Today, the Micmacs are one of the largest tribes east of the Mississippi River. There are over 12,000 Micmacs in New England with an additional 7000 in the Maritimes. About 900 Micmacs live in Maine, mostly in the potato growing area of Aroostook county.

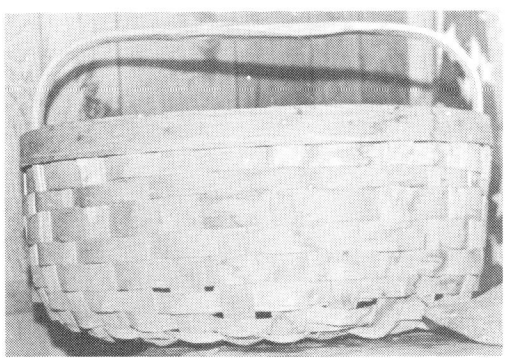

Old ash-splint potato basket. $35, Maine antique shop, fall 1986.

Well-made ash-splint basket, Unity College collection, NPA.

Hong Kong grass and ash-splint box. 5½" dia, 3⅜" h. $20, Maryland antique shop, fall 1986.

Covered ash-splint and sweet-grass box. 4" dia, 2½" h. $23, Connecticut antique shop, fall 1986.

The Micmacs were long considered a migratory tribe who "followed the fish." They've always had their own language and culture, and they are skilled basketmakers.

Basketmaking was essential in the early days for migratory people without paper bags, boxes, or trunks. For that reason, they learned how to make heavy burden baskets as well as lightweight "moving" baskets. They also made any other containers one might need including cooking and storage containers. Many of these were made of birch bark tied with spruce root. They made bags by weaving flat strips of the soft inner bark of cedar and basswood trees.

They used basswood in many ways. The strips of bark could be rolled into cords and later woven into baskets and mats. Oftentimes, they made twine of Indian hemp and used it with the bark of trees and with reeds. They made baskets of bark, roots, rush, and tough grasses, but today they are probably better known for their ash-splint baskets—the finer ones made of paper-thin splints and woven with sweet grass, their porcupine quill baskets and boxes. To make porcupine quill boxes they had to pluck the quills from dead porcupines, dye them, and then insert them in a design in birch-bark boxes. They also made baskets and boxes entirely of birch

Sweet-grass and ash-splint container, opens in middle, Unity College collection, NPA.

Ash-splint basket made to hold one-quart milk bottle. Private collection, NPA.

bark, and then scratched off part of the outer bark to make a design, or they painted a design.

The Micmacs still make potato-gathering baskets, but the demand is very low—now that machinery is used for the gathering. It's difficult to attribute certain baskets to any one tribe since the baskets are so similar among the many different tribes.

Milk Bottle Basket

Through the years, many wine and beverage bottlers, as well as individuals, have encased bottles in basketry. It's doubtful though, that too many people made a basket just to fit a one-quart milk bottle. The bottle basket shown here is believed to be one of a kind. It was made by a Penobscot Indian lady for her son's use when bringing home a quart of milk. Her son still remembers how he left the basket at the store in the morning on his way to school and picked it and the milk up on his way home in the afternoon. Later, she made one to fit a half-gallon bottle or jug, but no one knows what happened to it.

Milkweed

Milkweed grows wild over much of the country. It has a milky juice; hence, the name. There are two species that work well in basketry: One is the white milkweed, the other is red milkweed. In basketry, their stems are beaten until they separate into silky fibers, and then they are twisted into two-strand cords that can be used like sweet grass for weaving baskets. When twisted, the cord becomes very tough, yet remains pliable. When red and white milkweed are twisted together, they make a beautiful red and white rope. Shredded milkweed also makes a soft foundation material for coiled baskets.

Mill Baskets

Baskets were used in northern mills, but it is difficult to tell which type of basket was in which type of mill—cotton, silk, or woolen mills. The two baskets shown here were used in different mills, or at least for different chores. Oldtimers say these baskets were used in mills to transport various materials like thread, yarn, and finished fabric from one department to another. They are almost as large as the old balloon baskets, but are more closely woven. Made of willow, mill baskets are really too large to be collectible, except for nostalgic purposes.

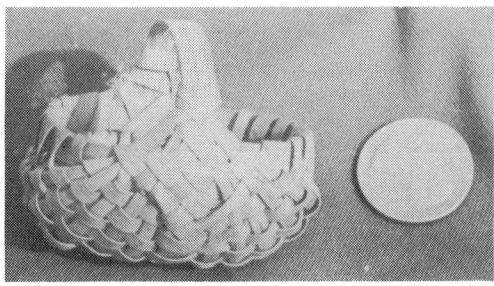

An oak-splint basket shown next to a quarter to indicate its size. Private collection, NPA. Old.

Two mill baskets, $20 each, Maine auction, fall 1986.

Finely woven miniature oak-splint baskets: (left) 1½" dia, 2" h, $25; (right) 2" dia, 3" h, $50, Nashville flea market, spring 1985. Old.

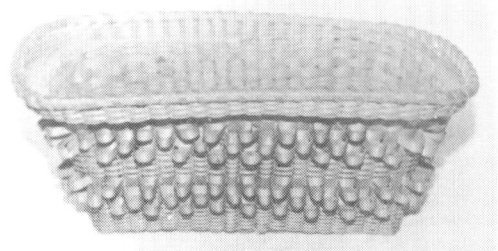

Ash-splint basket, use unknown, Unity College collection, NPA.

(left) River-cane Choctaw-made basket, 1½" dia, 3" h, $5, new; (right) three choctaw-made bead baskets, ½" dia, 1" h, $3 each, Choctaw reservation, spring 1986.

Miniature Baskets

Making of miniature baskets seems to intrigue old basketmakers as much as making novelties and oddities. They make miniature baskets using many different materials. The variety of miniature baskets includes a tiny Indian-made bead basket measuring only one-half inch in diameter to less than one inch in height. The Choctaws make a cane basket with a lovely dyed design that measures 1½ inches in diameter and 3 inches in height. Both the Cherokees and the Indians of the Northeast make sweet-grass and splint baskets just as small. They take great pride in making tiny baskets with tiny stitches. In fact, 40 stitches per inch is average on some of their small baskets, and some even have as fine as 60 to 70 stitches per inch.

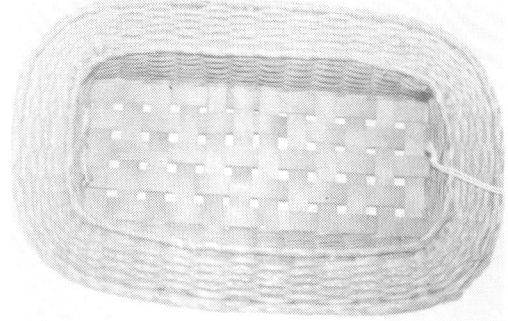

Open-weave bottom with sweet-grass flange, use unknown, Unity College collection, NPA.

Two similar baskets made of vine; probably fruit baskets. White, 11" dia, 6" h; natural 10" w, 13" l, 5" h, $10 each, Maine antique mall, 1986.

Miscellaneous Baskets

This category includes baskets still being researched. In some cases, the materials used to make them are known; for others, only the use or what is believed to have been the use of the basket is known. The following baskets are included here to show the types of baskets being offered today in antique shops, shows, and malls.

Oak-splint basket, use unknown. 18" dia, 13" h, $75, Texas antique shop 1986.

*Factory-made oak-splint basket, use unknown, 12" square, 15" o.h., **$50**, Texas antique shop, 1986.*

*Vine waste basket. 11½" dia, 7½" h, appears to be oriental. **$15**, Louisiana antique shop, 1986.*

Square, brightly colored, ash-splint covered basket, use unknown, Unity College collection, NPA.

*Factory-made oak-splint basket, use unknown, 20" square, 15" h, **$75**, Missouri antique shop, 1986.*

*Appears to be made of some kind of grass, and could be child's purse. 4" dia, 3½" h. **$15**, Maine antique shop, 1987.*

113

Colorful twined mat believed to have been made by one of the western Indian tribes. $75, New Hampshire mall, 1986.

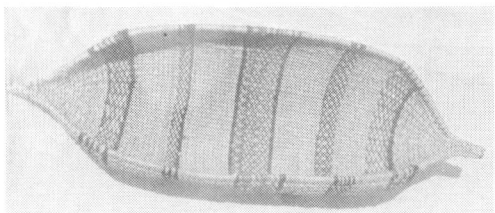

Colorful oblong woven tray, appears to be made of some type of heavy fiber, use unknown. 6" w, 20" l, 4" h. $18, Maine antique shop, 1986.

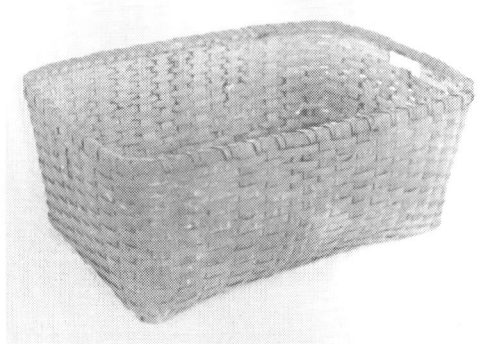

Small ash-splint basket painted dark red on the ends and sides; the rest is natural. Could have been some type of harvesting basket, or a small laundry basket. 12½" w, 19" l, 7½" h. $48, Maine antique show, fall 1986.

Work similar to that by Mission Indians. 11½" dia, 5½" h. $75, Pennsylvania antique shop, 1986.

Mission Indians

In the early days, the Mission Indians were prolific basketmakers. Their materials (which were mostly sumac and rush) and their weaves were limited. The Mission Indians' baskets were influenced by the Franciscan friars who controlled the missions of California. Friars supplied them with manufactured utensils, eliminating the need for much basketmaking.

In the early days, their work may have been of better quality, but in later years they used a coarser construction, with four to eight stitches per inch considered common.

Mohawk Indians

The Mohawks were part of the powerful Five Nations (comprised of Oneidas, Onandagas, Cayugas, Mohawks, and Senecas) that controlled most of what is now northern New York, southern Ontario, portions of Pennsylvania, and Ohio.

During the eighteenth century, the Tuscaroras joined this group to form Six Nations, making it even more powerful. The Six Nations became so powerful and so well organized, they were apt to declare war on anyone who threatened their territory.

Drum purse believed to have been made by the Mohawks. 8" dia, 3" h. $50, Maine auction, 1986.

Ash-splint yarn basket with two rows of Hong Kong grass, bottom and top. 6½" dia, 10" h. $35, Maryland mall, fall 1986.

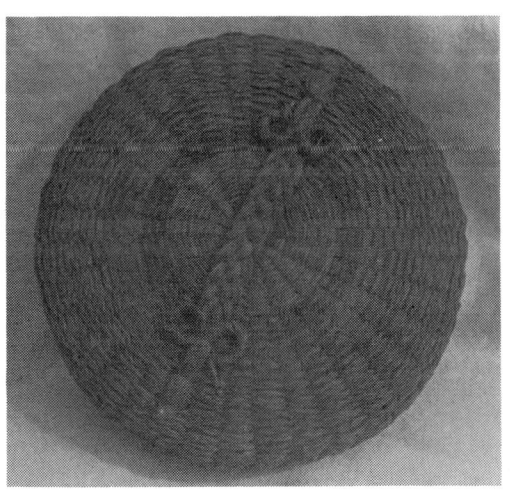

Top of covered ash-splint and sweet-grass basket, braided frog handle. 10" dia, 4" h. $38, Connecticut mall, 1986.

Squatty yarn basket, ash splint and Hong Kong grass. 7" dia, 6½" h. $48, Vermont mall, fall 1986.

The Mohawks were less nomadic than most tribes as they settled into houses—well-built houses with gabled roofs—and they were farming people. They had large, well-tended cornfields and larger than average vegetable gardens. For meat, they depended on hunting and fishing and were very skilled with their long, flat bows and bone fishhooks.

Since they stayed in one area, they could have more household utensils. They had items like wooden bowls, trays, spoons, and mortars and pestles, and they had an abundance of fine baskets.

Baskets found today, and known to have been made by Mohawks, are usually the tourist type, very similar to those made by New England tribes. They also used ash splints and sweet grass for most of their baskets. Some of the older Mohawk baskets are darker than those known to have been made in New England, but this could stem from the fact they used the heart of the ash, which is naturally darker.

Unless the provenance is known, it's easy to assign baskets made by one tribe to another.

Moose-Hair Embroidery

Moose-hair embroidery, like so many other tedious chores of the past, seems to be a lost art form. In 15 years of searching, this author has found only one moose-hair embroidered piece. The one shown here is the only one in the over 500-item Terry collection at Unity College, Unity, Maine. The late Mr. Terry studied and taught Indian culture, and collected Indian-made baskets for years, but found only this one embroidered with moose hair. Perhaps the task was so tedious and time-consuming, it was not practiced on a large scale.

Writing about the art of moose-hair embroidery, in 1932, Fannie Hardy Eckstorm in her book, *The Handicrafts of the Modern Indians of Maine,* said she was convinced that the work was done by the Huron Indians of Canada, as opposed to the theory that it was by the Penobscots. She based her theory on the fact that her father had a large trading post at Old Town,

Small, round birch-bark box with moose-hair embroidery. Terry Collection, Unity College, NPA.

Maine, during the 1870s, where he employed Penobscots to tan moose hides and then cut moccasins from them. Eckstorm's father left records stating that in 1872 he hired a Huron Indian who was visiting Old Town to help with the tanning and cutting. The Huron saved the long white hair he found on the throats of the winter-killed moose. He saved the white hair but returned the brown hair that was shaved off the moose hides. At that time, brown moose hair sold for around ten cents a pound in Maine, while the long white hairs brought as much as two dollars a pound in Quebec, where it was used for moose-hair embroidery.

As soon as Eckstorm's father learned that the Canadian Hurons were skilled in moose-hair embroidery, he sent the long white moose hair and the cut-out moccasins to them to be embroidered. When they were returned, the Penobscots sewed them together.

It's nearly impossible to imagine how the beautiful embroidery was accomplished with only long hairs from the neck of a moose, but it is exquisite. Some of the hairs were dyed in brilliant hues of green, red, yellow, and purple, and were used with the white to make designs—floral designs in the case of the box.

Mori-Kago

The Japanese name for a gift fruit basket is *mori-kago*. There was a time when gift giving flourished in Japan, and one of the most popular gifts was a basket of fresh fruit. As usual, the Japanese were concerned with the appearance of their gifts and made baskets best suited for the types of fruit each basket would contain. Oftentimes, the baskets were more valuable than the fruit.

Morita Skintaro

A Kyoto basketmaker who gained quite a reputation for his bamboo baskets. One of the secrets of his fine basketry was the fact he lived in an area that grew some of the finest, tallest, and straightest bamboo.

Mulberry

The mulberry tree served dual roles in American life. The flexible branches and shoots have long been recognized as good basketry material; like willow branches, those from the mulberry can be split to make fine weavers. The leaves were used as food for silkworms.

Mystery Basket

Even the most advanced collectors occasionally find something that defies rhyme and reason. That was the case with the basket we have elected to designate a mystery basket. There isn't a problem with the basket, itself, as it's a coiled Indian-made basket approximately a hundred years old. The mystery evolved when the basket was opened—there among the yellowed tissues was a paper-thin, porcelain-covered cup and saucer believed to be a rice cup. Judging by the way it fit into the tissues and basket, the china must have been in the basket for a long time. The question is: How did the china and the basket get together? Perhaps years ago some one put the china in the basket and gave it as a gift. The recipient apparently never used it and, instead, packed it away and forgot about it.

Yucca-wrapped rush-covered basket with china. 6½" dia, 3¾" h. $75, estate sale, fall 1986.

Nest of three small Nantucket baskets. Private collection, but owner appraises them at $750 each, 1987.

Nantucket Lightship Baskets

The making of the woven basket that would become known as the Nantucket Lightship basket began around 1850. The majority of these baskets were either round or oval in shape with wooden bases and movable handles attached to a pair of ears. They were often made in sets of seven or eight, and those sets have become extremely scarce and expensive (the old ones, that is). They are still being copied, and even the new ones are commanding high prices.

Rather than try to build a much-needed lighthouse, an impossible task, it seemed, at the time, a lightship was anchored off the shore of the tiny Nantucket Island in Massachusetts. Several sailors were always on board to keep the light burning. Tours of duty on the light ship were usually eight months long, so the sailors began making baskets to avoid the boredom—and they developed their own style.

The baskets became so popular, they began to be copied shortly after the first ones were shown. To differentiate between those actually made by the sailors and those made by basketmakers in the area, requires an expert. Those made by the lightship sailors (up until around 1895) and those made by others, including some of the retired sailors, are now selling at five-figure prices when found in well-preserved nested sets.

The demand for this type basket has been persistent and remains so, even today. Several modern basketmakers continue to make Nantucket Lightship-style baskets. A set of seven new nested baskets copied after the Nantucket lightship style, sold at a Maine auction, in 1985, for $1,400. New ones can be found all over New England, and most are sold as single baskets, rather than nested, with prices ranging from $200 to $300 for the smaller sizes, up to $500 or more for the larger ones.

Medium-sized Nantucket basket, private collection, NPA.

Note the wooden bottom in this Nantucket basket.

The Nantucket area had long been famous for whaling, but with the discovery of petroleum and kerosene, whale oil was no longer essential. Thus, whaling became much less important.

Nantucket Lightship-Type Purses

Around 1940, a Filipino decided to copy the old Nantucket baskets, making a smaller version. He added a top and made a lady's purse. The basket-purses became an instant success—so successful, in fact, that others began to copy the style. At first, these baskets were considered a fad or a novelty, but during the past few years they have become very collectible.

Early Nantucket-type basket-purse with the maker's name handpainted on the disc, private collection, NPA.

The Nantucket Lightship-type purse has a wooden base, like the baskets, and the lid has a small wooden disc, usually with some kind of decoration on it. Often, the decoration is a carved fish or bird, or a handpainted design. Many will have the name or intials of the maker. Older ones are now showing up in antique shops, shows, and malls in New England, with prices ranging from $95 for less-than-perfect examples, to as much as $300 for perfect ones. In other areas they may be priced higher. In fact, some contemporary basketmakers are now making their own versions of the basket purses; finer examples are priced in the $500 range.

Napkin Rings

The Victorian housewife was as fussy about her household linens as the Colonials were about their feather and down beds. There were few places to entertain guests outside the home, so she took great pride in snowy white tablecloths and napkins, which were always ironed to perfection. The napkins could be placed in a folded position on the table, folded into an ornate shape, or rolled and placed in napkin rings. Napkin rings were made in silver, cut glass, ivory, and heaven knows what other materials,

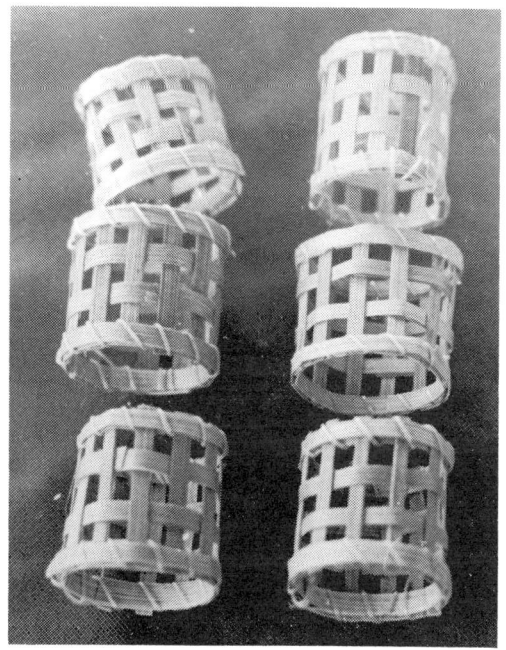

Set of six napkin rings. Variations in the size of each indicate an amateur basketmaker. $5 set, Mississippi antique shop, 1986.

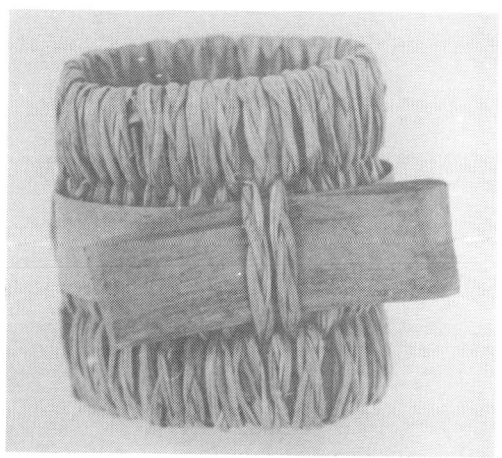

Sweet-grass napkin ring with ash-splint bow. $3.50, Maine antique show, fall 1986.

but the ones of more interest to basket collectors are the ones made of cane and grasses.

Cane napkin rings could have been made by southern basketmakers who had access to cane. There is little doubt that most of the sweet-grass napkin rings were made by basketmakers of the Northeast.

Another type of sweet-grass napkin ring. Unity College collection, NPA.

Two baskets made by Navajo instruction-book directions: (left) 10" dia, 3½" h, $60, New Hampshire mall; (right) 8" dia, 2½" h, $55, Vermont mall, fall 1986.

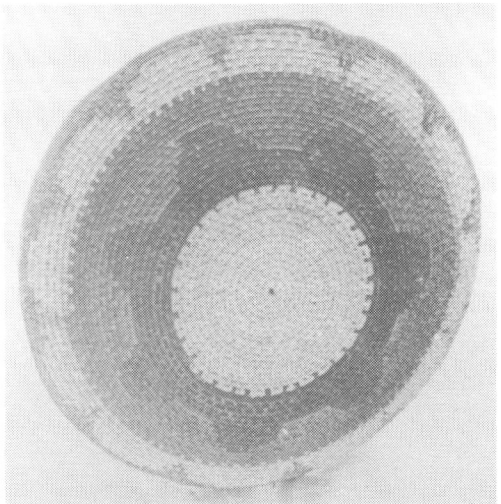

Colorful basket by Navajo instructions. 10" dia, 3" h, $45, Connecticut mall, fall 1986.

Covered basket by Navajo instructions. 10" dia, 4" h. $75, New Hampshire mall, fall 1986.

Navajo Basket-Weaving Book

Indian Basket Weaving was published by the Navajo School of Indian Basketry in 1903. It contained about 100 pages of instructions for making baskets exactly as the Indians made them, along with photos of fine, old Indian-made baskets. At least 20 different weaves were explained in simple enough detail that anyone could follow the instructions. Information was given on various materials, as well as all the necessary instructions on sizes and splicing.

The book was advertised in women's magazines. By following its instructions, a person could make replicas of baskets made by the western Indians. Apparently, a great number of baskets were made; they are now appearing in antique shops, shows, and malls, and are labeled "Indian baskets."

Purists will argue that these baskets were made only by western Indian designs. Those searching desperately for an example of these old baskets made *after* the western-Indian style welcome the chance to buy them for one tenth the price of the original. The baskets are well made; colorful, but faded; and they are old. Most appear to have been made of vine or rush, tightly woven with raffia.

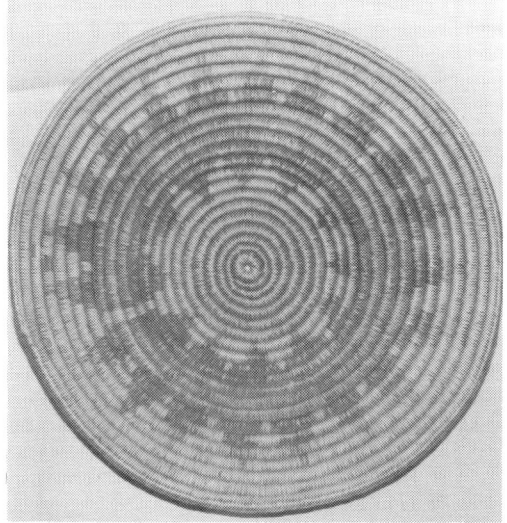

Old Navajo wedding basket. Terry Collection, Unity College, NPA.

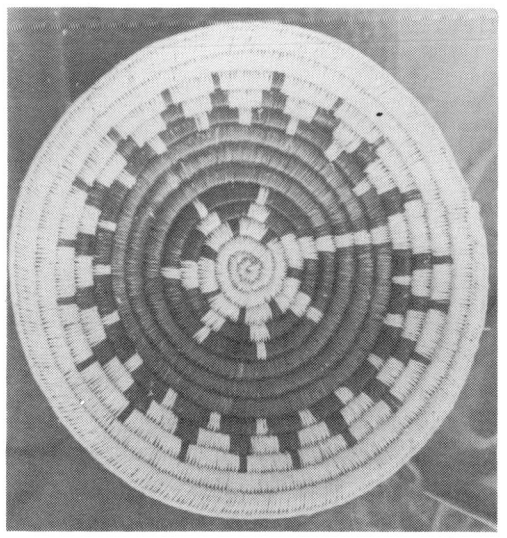

New Navajo wedding basket. 13" dia. $175, arts and crafts store on reservation, 1986.

Navajo Indians

The Navajos (along with the Apaches) began moving southward from Canada around the thirteenth century. They always moved southwesterly, heading for Arizona. Their name, also spelled Havaho, means "large cultivated fields." They called themselves Dine, pronounced dih-NAY, the people. Today, they're one of the largest tribes in the States with approximately 160,000 members. About 110,000 live on the 16-million acre reservation in Arizona.

Baskets have been a part of the Navajo culture for so long, they're even mentioned in the Navajo Origin myth. During that time, the men and women began considering living separate lives. Before they could do that, however, the man had to consider whether or not he could handle the woman's chores such as cooking, making pottery, and most important, making baskets.

From the very beginning, the Navajos made burden baskets, water jugs, and other types of baskets, including the famous wedding basket. Generally, their baskets were made with a twined weave, using a three-rod foundation woven with sumac.

Baskets were always essential to Navajo tribal ceremonies, but no other type of basket was used more than the wedding basket. It was, and still is used for serving cornmeal mush at weddings and as a receptacle for sacred items, and it was sometimes used as a drum.

Gathering sumac for the Navajo baskets was similar to gathering cane for baskets made by the Choctaws and Cherokees. They first went to the fields where sumac grew and crawled around among the sumac bushes to find just the right kinds of branches. Then, once the branches were taken home, the Navajos tore them apart with their hands and teeth, much like the process used on cane. Sumac branches came apart in three pieces, and were allowed to dry thoroughly before being rubbed with buckskin to remove the parts not needed in the basketry.

Only three colors were ever used to make the Navajo wedding baskets—red, white, and black. Roots of mountain mahaghony were used to make red dye. Once the sumac had been cleaned and dyed, it was time to begin making the basket.

It took patience and endurance to make a Navajo wedding basket and only experienced basketmakers were allowed to make wedding baskets. (It took about three years to become experienced.)

After the white man came, the Navajos began using more metal containers, and so basket production slowed considerably. They continued to make baskets—a craft they continue today, but they were not as dependent on baskets after the white man came.

Then, restrictions were imposed on the Navajos making baskets—restrictions so complicated, many Navajo women stopped making them altogether. In fact, production decreased so badly between the 1920s and 1950s, the Navajos were forced to buy some of their baskets from Ute and Paiute basketmakers. This helps to explain the scarcity of old Navajo baskets.

This situation has changed considerably in recent years. One reason for this is the demand for baskets, new or old, and with that demand has come better prices—prices high enough to encourage Navajo women to resume basketmaking.

Navaho Indians

Another spelling for Navajo. See Navajo Indians.

New Philippine Baskets

So many new baskets are coming from the Philippines now, it's difficult to keep up with them. Women in many areas are having "basket parties" on the order of the plastics and cosmetics parties. They go to each other's homes where they play games and see displays of the new baskets for sale.

This small basket is a new Papago-made; the large one was newly made in the Philippines.

Most of the baskets seen have labels stating they were made "exclusively for home parties," and in smaller letters that they were made in the Philippines. The baskets are well made and inexpensive when compared to the finer, old baskets. Of course, this is one of the best arguments for studying all types of baskets before spending large sums of money. These baskets can be aged a bit on the outside, and it is going to be a tad difficult to separate them from some of the newer, expensive ones being made by the Indians of the Southwest, such as the one shown in the illustration here. The larger basket was made recently in the Philippines and sold at a basket party for $5. The smaller one was made recently by the Papago Indians and retails for $75. There is quite a difference between the two when you study them carefully, but at a glance, they seem quite similar.

Nootka Indians

Although they live in British Columbia, the Nootkas have always been closely associated with the Makahs—probably due to the fact both are experienced whalers and work in the same area. The baskets made by the two tribes are so similar, it is almost impossible to distinguish between them. Collectors seldom try; they simply lump them together.

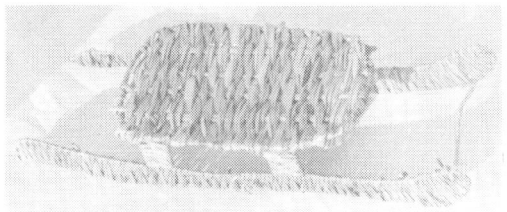

Nootka basket, private collection, NPA.

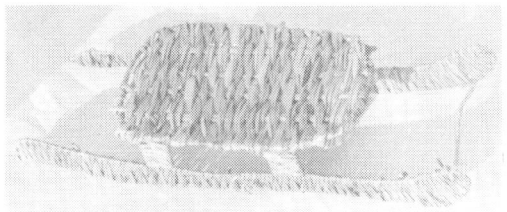

Woven grass sled. 6" w, 16" l. $15, Maine antique shop, 1987.

New Penobscot rocking-chair pin cushion, sweet grass and ash splint. 3½" w, 4" h. $18, from maker, 1987.

Novelties in Basketry

Many of the small items like miniature baskets and animal effergies could be classed as novelties, but they fit better in their individual categories. Therefore, only a couple of basketry items will be included in novelties: the grass sled, and the sweet-grass rocking chair pin cushion.

Small, sturdy oak-splint basket, private collection, NPA.

Oak Splints

There are 22 two different species of oak tree in this country, and probably only a few of them are excellent for making splints for baskets. Most people would describe oak splints as "made of white oak." The people living in the mountains, both Great Smoky and Ozarks, prefer white oak, and they use it extensively. It works up easily, makes a beautiful basket, and judging by the number still available, is one of the more durable splints. They can be cut very fine or can be left wide and thick to make burden baskets.

Half-bushel oak-splint basket, private collection, NPA.

Round oak-splint basket. 16" dia, 22" o.h. $250, Maine estate auction, 1986.

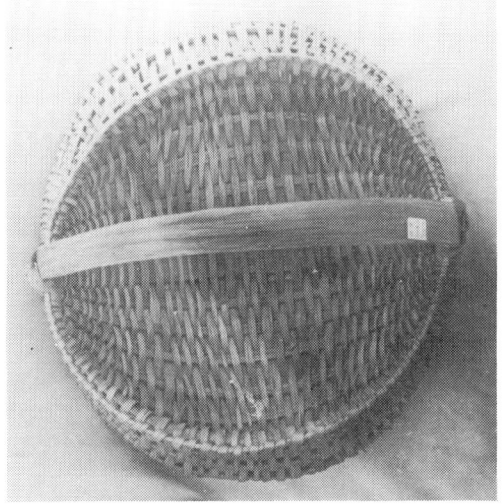

Very popular oak-splint gizzard or buttocks basket. 12" dia, 14" o.h. $300, Missouri antique shop, 1986.

Small oak-splint basket. 10" dia, 11" h. $39, Maine auction, fall 1986.

Oak-splint basket filled with apples. 12" dia, 12" h. $57, Maine auction, fall 1986.

Old unusual-shaped basket attributed to the Penobscots, ash splints. Unity College collection, NPA.

Two old oak-splint baskets made in the Great Smoky Mountains. Private collection, NPA.

Old swamp-cane basket attributed to the Choctaws. 12" w, 18" l, 13" o.h. $95, Mississippi antique shop, 1986.

Obijwa Indians

Original name for the tribe now known as Chippewa. First settlers corrupted their name. See Chippewa.

Ogawa Hihei

A Japanese basketmaker who lived and worked in Osaka. His work was as famous and sought after in Japan as some of the better basketmakers in America.

Open Baskets

The style of basket and whether or not it had a lid depended, in part, on how it would be used. Most egg and market baskets were left open since they were used daily by the owner. If the basket was going to be used as a picnic or lunch basket, it generally had a lid.

Old Cherokee cane basket. $225, North Carolina antique shop, 1986.

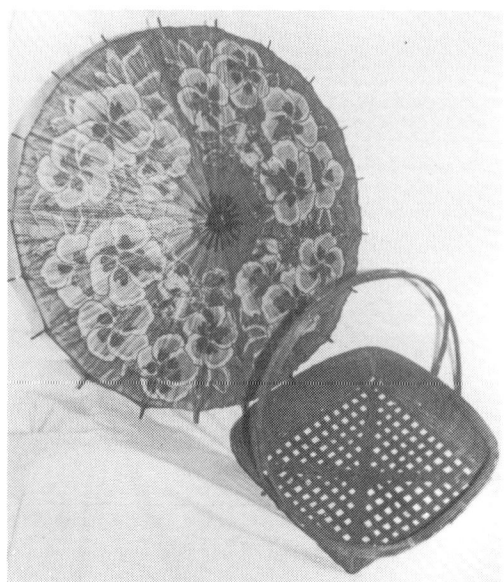

Bamboo basket with paper umbrella. 12" square, 12" o.h. $25, Florida mall, 1986.

Baskets that were to be used for storage had covers to keep out mice, squirrels, and anything else that might eat the food and grain stored in the basket. Mice and squirrels could eat their way through thin splints, so basketmakers soon devised a way to combat the problem—they used thicker splints and, in some cases, owners would tie the baskets to the ceiling.

Oriental Baskets

Although Oriental baskets are as old and as well made as other baskets, they've never sold for prices like other baskets. Recently, however, demand and price for these baskets have been increasing. One reason for the Oriental basket's previous lack of popularity could be the influx of cheap baskets into this country before World War II, and more recently, the number of new baskets coming in from China and the Philippines.

A reason for the increasing popularity could be that many displaced Vietnamese are now making baskets, and since we realize that they make baskets by hand, just as our ancestors did, their baskets are more desirable.

This is believed to be an old, willow Oriental purse. $35, Maine auction, fall 1986.

Some of the older Oriental baskets were considered cheap and were sold in dime stores, and yet the opposite was often true—some were of excellent quality and workmanship.

As early as the turn of the twentieth century, some people were trying to interest collectors in the beauty of Oriental basketry. One writer wrote that Oriental baskets were excellent examples of workmanship and were very artistically made.

Bamboo wastebasket of the 1920s with a painted design around the sides. 12" dia, 13" h. $15, Maine mall, 1987.

Late bamboo wastebasket; note the bamboo-stalk legs. 16" dia, 14" h. $15, Maine antique show, 1987.

They were made as "objects of utility rather than as works of art," he wrote, "but the artistic element was introduced as the work progressed."

Oriental baskets, like teakwood furniture, were made more elaborate for the American market, which is what the Oriental basketmakers believed we wanted.

The majority of Oriental basketry was made of bamboo, although various vines, rattan, and willow were also used. Bamboo and other materials were used to make handbags, cigar and cigarette cases, tobacco pouches, lunch boxes, sewing baskets, and all types of fruit and flower baskets, and later, wastebaskets.

Ox Muzzles

Chances are, woven muzzles were used more on calves than on grown oxen. Muzzles were used to keep young calves from nursing their mothers for too long. In other words, muzzles were used to wean them. Plow horses and oxen were muzzled to keep them from nibbling on crops—particularly young corn. Most muzzles resembled the horse-feeding basket, but were made with loosely woven bottoms—if the animals had to wear them for long periods of time, this design allowed them to breath the fresh air more easily than did a regular horse feeding basket.

Painted Baskets

Since baskets have become so popular as decorative accessories, and prices have spiraled accordingly, many ingenious people have begun buying and painting the old, cheap, factory-made baskets. Some are simply painted in bright colors, while others have designs added. A long time ago, this ordinary basket (next page) was painted a rich green, and then a gold-leaf design of leaves and vines was added. Red dots were placed here and there to make it look like holly for a Christmas basket.

Factory-made basket painted and decorated. 6" w, 18" l, 10" o.h. $9, New England flea market, 1986.

New Paiute tray in red and natural. 11" dia. $80, Navajo craft store, Arizona, 1986.

Paiute Indians

The Paiute Indians have long been famous for their basketry. They have made some of the finest baskets, including their beaded baskets. Unlike some of the western Indians, who would sew and weave bead designs into their baskets, the Paiutes would fasten their bead designs on the basket's top.

The Paiutes are part of the Shoshone group that is also famous for fine basketry. Most Paiute baskets were made in four colors—black, brown, red, and yellow.

Palmetto

Several species of palms growing in the southeastern part of the United States are lumped under the name palmetto, but only the Afro-American or Gullah people of the Low Country of South Carolina know the best ones to gather for their baskets.

All of the palms have served the people well. The wood of the cabbage palm is valued for its hardness and durability; the leaves of this palm, as well as those of other palm trees, are used to make hats, fans, and lacings for Gullah baskets.

The Afro-Americans gather the palmetto and place it in water for a short time. Then, after the palmetto is cut or torn into strips, they put it in the freezer for several weeks, which they say makes it work easier and better, and look better.

Palm Leaves

Palm leaves were used to make the clutch purse shown here. This type of purse was made in Hawaii before World War II, and possibly afterwards. It's made of coconut palm fronds in a checkerboard design. Palm leaves were also used to make hats, fans, and other woven items during that time. They were made in Florida and Cuba as well as South Carolina.

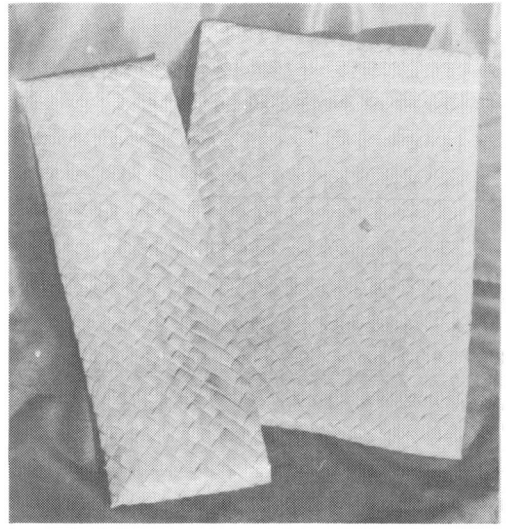

Clutch purse c. 1940, made of palm leaves. 9 ½" w, 13" l, $5, Maine antique show, 1986.

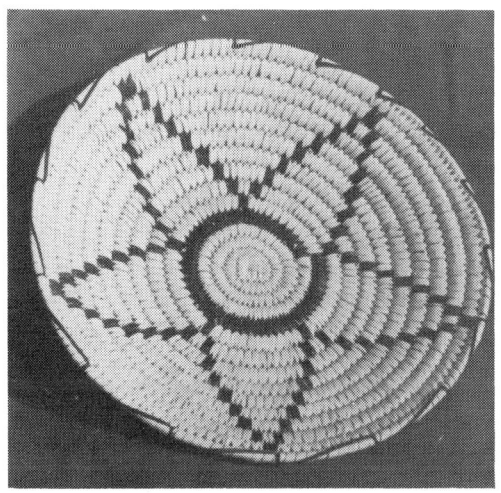

New Papago basket, Yucca and devil's claw. 10" dia. $75, Arizona gift shop, 1986.

Basket with cane spokes, paper weavers, and a twisted vine handle. 7" w, 9½" l, 8" h. $12, New England antique mall, fall 1986.

Papago Indians

The Papagos are close relatives of the Pimas. Because of their need to find water they can be described as seminomadic.

The men did the farming while the women gathered cactus fruit, mesquite beans, and other wild growing foods to supplement their meager harvest. If there wasn't enough rain to produce the crops they needed, they moved on.

Papago is a Pima word meaning *Bean People* and it was acquired from their dependence on beans—cultivated beans when they could get them, Mesquite beans when they could not.

The Papagos are still making baskets just as they have been for centuries. But today the newly made baskets are grabbed up by collectors rather than used by the Indians. The Papagos still use the same methods and materials: yucca and devil's claw. Old Papago baskets can be found from time to time, but they aren't plentiful.

Paper Rope Basketry

A paper rope basket immediately conjures up visions of Oriental baskets, probably paper rice baskets. But paper baskets were made in this country by women who became involved in the basketry revival of the 1920s. It was around 1920 that Dennison Manufacturing Company published a 32-page booklet of instructions for making all types of paper and wire baskets, trays, and even lamp shades.

To make the spokes, crepe paper was twisted around small wires. More crepe paper was twisted into ropes for weavers. The booklet listed a dozen different weaves including Japanese single weave, pineapple, and arrowhead triple weave. Directions were given for making all types of baskets, including a heart shaped and a sandwich basket. It also included directions for making a lamp base to be used with the paper rope shade. Any of the instructions could have been converted to use with other materials.

Pea Basket

In the Deep South where field peas and black-eyed peas grow in profusion, an oak splint basket known as a *pea basket* was once used. These were made in assorted sizes—apparently to fit the needs of the picker. Although similar baskets were made and used in other areas, and were called by other names, the southern pea basket was known for its taller handle, allowing the basket to be carried on the arm while leaving enough room for peas to be placed in it with no effort. The sides of the

Old pea basket painted white. 12" w, 18" l, 15" o.h. $55, south Alabama antique shop, spring 1986.

Old peat basket made of splints, private collection, NPA.

Old porcupine quill box thought to have been made by the Penobscots. 3½" w, 5" l, 2½" h. $85, Maine mall, 1986.

basket had to be just right—low enough to allow the peas to be put inside with little or no effort, yet high enough that the peas wouldn't fall out when the picker bent over to pick more.

Peat Basket

Long ago in Europe, peat, a partially decayed, moisture-absorbing plant matter found in old peat bogs and swamps, was used as fuel for heating homes. The peat had to be dug, then carried to the house—in a basket. The baskets were made large enough to accomodate quite a bit of peat, enough to keep the home fires burning for a while. The baskets were also used to bring in driftwood and dead limbs, and anything else used to keep the fires going. Out of necessity, these baskets had to be strong and sturdy. It is not unusual to find old books with pictures of ladies and their baskets of peat.

Penobscot Indians

It would be difficult to say which of the four tribes—Micmacs, Penobscots, Maliseets, or Passamaquoddies—living in Maine, makes the most or the best baskets. For centuries, they have all excelled in basketry. Many examples of their work can still be found, some of it absolutely exquisite. Penobscot women, who learned the art and craft of basketmaking from their mothers and grandmothers, are still making baskets. These women are also now teaching classes for those who want to learn basketmaking. For those who want to study the work and culture of the tribe, there is the Penobscot Indian Museum in Old Town, Maine.

New Penobscot-made yarn basket, ash splint and sweet grass. 7" dia, 11½" h. $50, Penobscot reservation, fall 1986.

Double-handled ash-splint basket. 4" dia, 5½" h. $18, New England auction, 1986.

Ash-splint covered basket. 14" dia, 10" h. $57, Maine antique show, 1986.

Penobscot-made work basket filled with ash splints, Unity College collection, NPA.

Covered ash-splint basket. 15" dia, 10" h. $65, Maine antique show, 1987.

The Penobscot Indian Nation is the oldest documented, continuously operating government in North America—a government that continues, today, with its unbroken succession of Chiefs and Governors.

The few very early examples of Penobscot work belongs to descendents of the makers; therefore, it's difficult to find items to compare with the baskets made later. But it would be safe to assume that both designs and colors were changed to meet the competition around the turn of the century when the Penobscots began making baskets for the tourist trade. They didn't change the quality—it is still excellent.

The Penobscots lived in the same area as the Shakers, who would often farm out basketmaking jobs to Indians, and they would make the baskets to Shaker specifications. The Penobscots were very skilled and had to depend, to some extent, on the money coming in from their baskets. Thus, it is safe to assume that they made many items for the Shakers, and also, they may have made extras of that type to sell to their customers.

The Shakers not only went into towns and resort areas selling their baskets and other items, they had community stores at their farms. The Penobscots had roadside stands and they sold at gift shops around the resorts.

Basketmaking hasn't changed much for the Penobscots in recent years, except that they have to travel further to find the fine ash trees required for their basketry. The men still go out and find the trees, cut them into lengths, and bring them home where they pound them to separate the annual growth. From there, it is usually the work of the women to finish preparing the materials and then make the baskets, although some men still make baskets. Gathering sweet grass is a job for either the men or the women, and either can comb it after it is dry. The men are usually the ones who make the sweet-grass combs and the molds or forms, and the cutters.

The Penobscots not only excel in ash-splint and sweet-grass basketry, they also make birch-bark and porcupine quill boxes. Their early work was so fine, an English visitor once wrote that they made "dishes of birch bark sewed with thread from spruce [spruce] and white cedar roots." The pieces were decorated with *florisht* work," he wrote, "like glittering quills from the porcupine." He also mentioned that they were dyeing the quills in various colors, verifying an early use of both porcupine-quill decoration and the use of dyes, as this was written in the mid 1600s.

Peruvian Weave

Actually, the Peruvian weave is a variation of the Lazy Squaw weave, one that was described as easy in most basketry books.

Lazy squaw was the first weave described in the Indian basket-weaving book published in 1903. The only variation, they said, was the difference in the number of times the raffia was wound around the reed before the stitch was caught under the previous row. They suggested using raffia rather than the material used by the Navajo women. By varying the number of times the raffia was wound between the stitches, different designs and effects could be produced. The more raffia one used, the stronger the basket.

In some places, these raffia-covered reed baskets are sold as Indian-made. A few may be Indian-made, but the majority were made by women who followed instructions given in basketry books that offered to send a kit with an "already begun" basket. The ladies could order the kits with the baskets already started, and then complete them and have what they considered to be Indian baskets. They would tell their families and friends they had genuine Indian baskets, and that myth continues today.

Two variations of the Peruvian weave were the diamond pattern and the spiral pattern.

Small raffia-covered reed box in Peruvian weave. Note the button on the inside—it is used to hold the finial. 8½" dia, 2¼" h. $45, Maine antique shop, fall 1986.

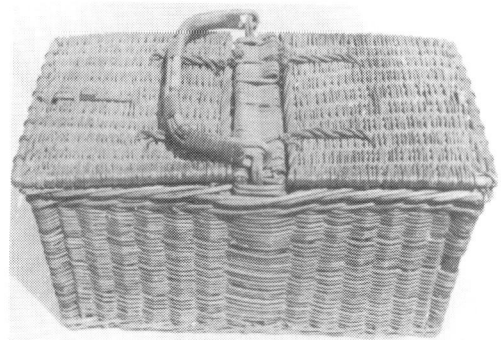

Intriguing willow picnic basket with primitive lid fastener. 11" w, 17" l, 8" h. $25 due to worn condition, Maine flea market, summer 1986.

Swing handle on a picnic basket.

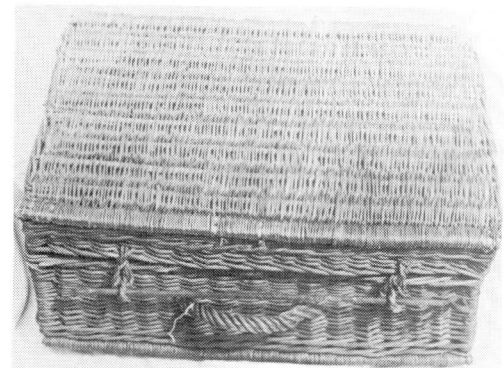

Flat willow picnic basket, private collection, NPA.

Philippine-Made Baskets

It's nearly impossible to tell which of the old baskets were made in the Philippines and which were made in other Oriental countries. But there is no problem with the new Philippine-made baskets. They have labels listing the country of manufacture, and they are coming to the States in greater and greater numbers. See New Philippine Baskets.

Picnic Baskets or Hampers

Like the sewing basket, picnic baskets were made in a variety of shapes and sizes. Many picnic baskets made after the introduction of the automobile were designed especially to be used with cars. In fact, at least one is known to have the name of the car, Renault, stenciled in the inside cover.

They were made of every conceivable material. Some were plain, actually on the primitive side, while the later ones came complete with dishes, flatware and woven bottle holders on the side. The fancy, fitted ones are still made today at one basket factory, and maybe at others as well.

During the first part of the twentieth century, picnicking was considered the perfect date for young couples. Since there were so few forms of entertainment—no radio or TV, few picture shows, and so forth—a picnic was considered the perfect place for a gentleman to take his date, which required a picnic basket.

Willow was one of the most popular picnic-basket materials, although many other kinds were used.

Woven-splint pie basket with mounted duck. 11" dia, 5" h. $15, Maine auction, fall 1986.

Double-handled Passamaquoddy-made pie basket. 12" dia, 12" h. $18, Maine auction, fall 1986.

Pie Basket

There weren't many bakeries years ago, so the housewife baked on her own. In fact, baking was one of the things she considered absolutely essential, and she never missed a chance to show off her baking skills.

She would pack her finest pies in a pie basket and off she went to the church gathering, family reunion, or picnic in the meadow. The pies might be sweet or meat, and they might be packed in single or double-decker pie baskets, with handles or without. They might have double handles and they could be open or covered, but the majority were covered. The type of pie basket, like all other baskets, seemed to depend on the needs and desires of the user. Pie baskets were also used for cakes, and sometimes they were used as storage places for cakes and pies in the home. The pie basket was probably the forerunner of the later metal, aluminum, and plastic cake and pie containers.

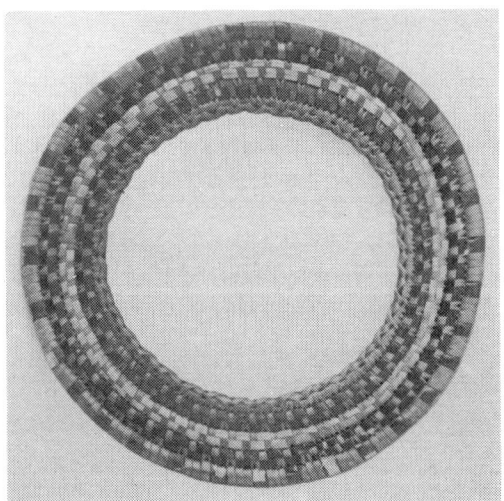

Picture frame woven of grass. 11" dia. $55, Vermont mall, fall 1986.

Picture Frame

Old woven picture frames are scarce, but later wicker ones are plentiful. The illustration dates around 1920 and is believed to have been made by the Eskimos of Alaska. The grass used to make it, and the workmanship, closely resemble Eskimo work. When found, this picture frame contained a religious picture and a notation on the back that it was a confirmation gift, apparently for a French Canadian as the message was in French and had a Canadian address.

Round rattan cushion (left), $12; sweet grass (right), $22, Maine antique mall, fall 1986.

Velvet-topped Shaker pincushion. $38, Maine antique show, 1987.

Pincushions

From their arrival on the Mayflower to the turn of the century, most American ladies made their own clothing or had them made by a dressmaker. This meant pins and needles were essential for everyone. Pins were not only essential, they were quite expensive for many years; thus, the housewife wanted to take care of the pins she had and wanted to know where to find them when she needed them. With that idea in mind, someone created the pincushion. Since they were handmade, they were made in many different styles and sizes, and of many materials. When basketry was at its peak of popularity, pincushions were made of rattan with padded velvet tops, and in the Northeast, they were made of ash splint with ribbon-bedecked satin tops. The Shakers made them using woven poplar.

Pine Bark Strips

There are dozens of different kinds of pine trees growing all over the world. One species may furnish food (nuts); another lumber for house- and ship-building; and another tar, turpentine, and resin. Other pine trees furnish bark that's perfect for cutting into thin strips for weaving and plaiting into basketry items. The cones off some trees are used to make wreaths for Christmas decorations, and some of the small green pine trees are used for Christmas trees. Needles from the long-leaf pine are used by both white and Indian basketmakers.

Pine Cones

Long-leaf pine needles are used to make baskets and other basketry items, and the beautiful little pine cones are used to decorate them, giving them an overall pine look. Some cones are left natural; others are painted bright colors before being attached to the pine needle or vine baskets.

New Coushatta pine needle basket decorated with small pine cones and green raffia leaves, 9½" dia, 8½" h. $35. Coushatta reservation, 1986.

Bottom of a fancy pine needle basket made by a white basketmaker.

Lined pine needle basket (bottom shown above). 10" dia, 3" h. $19, Maine flea market, fall 1986.

New Miccosukke pine needle basket with doll head finial. 9" dia, 7" h. $90, Florida gift shop, 1986.

Pine Needle Basketry

About 400 species of pine are known to grow all over the world, yet they have only been used extensively in the southern part of the United States to make basketry items. Only the long needle variety, those measuring 12 to 20 inches long, can be used. They are most easily found under the trees known as long-leaf or slash pine.

Both the Indian and white basketmakers in the southeastern part of the country have long made baskets and novelty items using pine needles. Pine needles can be gathered during any time of year, but to get the best quality with the least trouble, they should be gathered in the late spring or early summer, as soon as they have reached full growth. Some basketmakers wait until fall—usually late fall or early winter—and then gather the pine needles that have fallen. If they are left too long, however, they will become brittle and be difficult to work with.

Each basketmaker had his or her own method of gathering. Some prefer the fallen needles after they have turned brown, while others prefer using them while they are still a bit green. An 82 year old Coushatta man makes baskets while the needles are a bit green and uses no finish. I thought they might become loose after drying out completely, but a year later they were as tight as the day they were bought.

Early basketmakers stitched the coils of pine needles in their baskets with embroidery thread, a custom continued by the Miccosukee Indians in Florida. But most pine needle basketmakers today use raffia. It's also interesting that most white pine needle basketmakers finish their baskets with a solution of shellac, while Indians leave theirs natural.

Just as they have different ideas for gathering and finishing pine needle baskets, basketmakers have different methods for curing the needles. To get a rich brown color, the needles are left in the rain, sun, frost, and wind for as long as it takes for them to reach a rich, golden brown color. Or, if the basketmaker prefers green needles, as most Indian basketmakers do, they're left to dry away from the sun and rain, preferably in the house. Some makers remove the growth end of the needles, while others use them to an advantage in the design.

Pine Needle Stitches

Each basketmaker uses the stitches of his or her choice, but the basic pine needle stitches are plain, single split, wheat, leaf, wing, and fern.

Pitchers, Woven

No one has yet been able to explain why basketmakers wove pitchers unless it was to prove anything could be made in basketry. Or, perhaps novelties like pitchers sold well. Many basketmakers supplemented their meager incomes by selling baskets, which means they made things they thought would sell. They also copied items made by other basketmakers, but one of the quickest ways to start an argument is to ask an old basketmaker who made a certain basketry item first. Each basketmaker claims to be the first, whether they are white or Indian.

Oak-splint pitchers were made in the Great Smoky and Ozark mountain areas. Ash-splint and sweet-grass examples were made in the Northeast.

Oak-splint pitcher. 7" dia, 9" h. $200, North Carolina antique shop, 1986.

Ash-splint and sweet-grass pitcher. 4" dia, 6" h. Unity College collection, 1987.

Piticas

Double woven and lidded baskets of beargrass, made by the Tarahumara Indians of northern Mexico. See Tarahumara.

Plaiting

Basketmakers of the Northeast use plaiting, or braiding, to weave sweet grass into the beautiful designs they use on their ash-splint baskets. Among the Indian basketmakers, the Micmacs, Mohawks, and Passamaquoddies seem to opt for the use of plaited or braided sweet grass fastened on the outside of their basketry items, while the Penobscots, Chippewas, and some other tribes prefer to include the designs in the baskets themselves.

Plate, Basketry Covered

Quite often, plates are seen encased in a basketry holders—the back of a plate is completely covered and a basketry rim extends around the front. First impression links this to imported products—and some probably are—but during the first and second decades of this century, when basketry was experiencing such a revival, instructions were given in several books for "covering a plate with vine, willow, or reed."

Plunder Basket

No special basket was made for this purpose; any old basket will suffice. Plunder basket is simply the name given an old basket used to hold *plunder,* or as my grandmother described it, "things too good to throw away, yet not really good enough to keep." New baskets were seldom used as plunder baskets; instead, the beautiful old ones were relegated to this chore when they became too worn for their regular chores. My grandmother kept hers in the pantry of the old farm house.

Poarch Creek Indians

Like so many southern tribes, the Poarch were skilled in pine needle basketry, and also used some cane in earlier days. They no longer make baskets. They are now involved in business—a bingo palace that enables them to buy and operate motels, restaurants, low income housing, and a catfish processing plant—all near the reservation at Atmore, Alabama. With only 1800 Poarch left on the reservation, most of them are working on the various businesses, leaving little time for basketmaking.

Pomo Indians

A century ago, California boasted of 700,000 Indian inhabitants. Unlike other Indians, these people preferred the simple, peaceful life. Some were even described as lazy because they were content to utilize the available materials to fit their simple, everyday needs.

They all made baskets. Some like the Pomos made exquisite baskets—very desirable baskets with decorations of beads, feathers, and shells. More than two years were required to make some of their beautiful baskets, and they also made other types of baskets, some rather plain. In fact, the Pomos were among the most versatile basketmakers, as they could combine both twining and coiling in so many different ways.

Originally, their name was Poma, *Po* for red color and *Ma* for earth. They became known as "the people of the red earth," and then, the name was changed to Pomo.

Old willow-wrapped basket is similar to those made by the Pomos. 9½" dia, 7" h. $50, damaged condition, Rhode Island antique shop, fall 1986.

Ash-splint and sweet-grass basket with porcupine weave. 6½" dia, 3½" h. $29, Vermont flea market, 1986.

This style of work was introduced in the 1860s, but since the porcupine weave is difficult to do and is time-consuming, it has not been used as much in recent years. Old baskets with porcupine weave can be found quite often. Some are light in color, indicating they have been stored in attics and basements, shielded from air and light.

To make the porcupine weave, the basketmaker took both ends of a piece of paper-thin ash splint and turned them to the center. The next step was to roll the splint under, leaving a sharp point on the basket. The splint was passed under the weaver, given a sharp turn outward, another turn inward, and then passed under the next spoke. A plain weaver was worked along with it at the same time to keep the sides of the basket strong.

Finer quality ash-splint basket with smaller porcupine-weave design. 8" dia, 5½" h. $30, Maine auction, fall 1986.

New porcupine quill box. 4½" w, 5½" l, 3" h. $105, Maine maker, fall 1986.

Porcupine Weave or Design

Much confusion has arisen over the difference between porcupine weave or design and porcupine quill work. The former is a design created by curling ash splints into points, while the latter is when quills are removed from the porcupine and inserted into birch-bark boxes, belts, and other items.

Porcupine Quill Work

Porcupine quill work is sometimes called, simply, *quill work*. It can be compared to embroidery, as the quills from a porcupine are used to make a design on birch bark. That is, they are worked in to form a design.

New porcupine quill box shaped like a house, private collection, NPA.

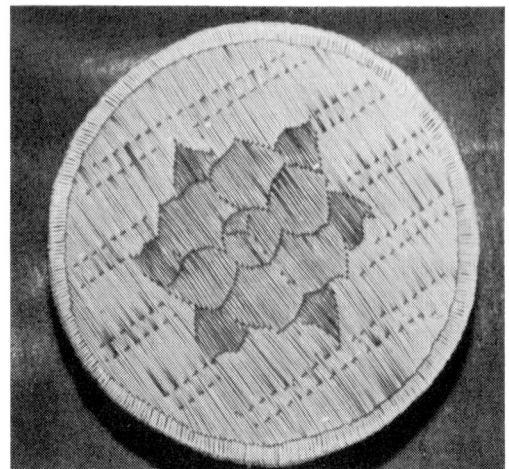

Porcupine quill box, Unity College collection, NPA.

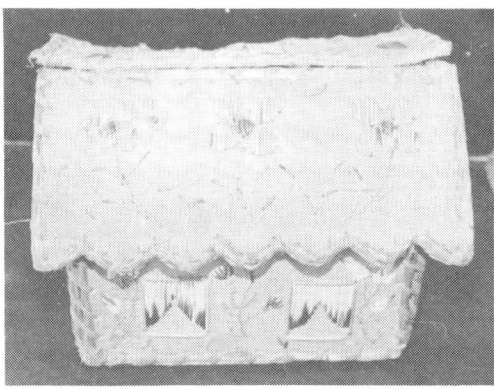

Side view of same box.

Old porcupine quill box. 4½" dia, 2½" h. $45 because of damaged condition, Maine antique mall, fall 1986.

The quills are removed from the dead porcupine and vary in length from 1½ to 3 inches. The quills can also vary in diameter, but only by fractions of an inch. They are hollow, which means they can be used round, crushed flat, or split.

The first chore after the quills are plucked is to dry them, and then sort and grade according to quality and length. Then, the quills are ready to be dyed. Surprisingly, porcupine quills can be dyed with the same vegetable dyes used in other basket materials. Today, porcupine-quill basketmakers use commercial dyes like all other basketmakers.

The Indians of the Northeast were the first to make quill boxes and baskets. Working with them is an art, and a rather difficult one to master as the quills can not be worked in a circle. The designs have to be made so the quills can be inserted either straight or in a geometric design. Flowers can be made, but the design has to be such that the quills are placed straight to form the round or pointed petals.

Since quill work is very tedious and can be painful when the workers' fingers continue to be pierced by the sharp quills, it has been practiced on a limited basis. The quills are very sharp and both ends have to be inserted into the birch bark. Workers can't wear gloves as they have to feel the quills working into place.

The birch bark is first cut to make whatever the maker wants, and then the quills are inserted into the design. Some makers are able to work with completed boxes, but most prefer doing the quill work, then completing the box—lacing it together with spruce roots or basswood.

Once the box is cut, the design to be used is decided; then, the design is sketched on the bark. Quill work can not be done on a by-guess-and-by-gosh method if it is to be attractive. When the sketch is done, small holes are punched into the bark with the small awl. The holes have to be very close together, and there must be two—one for either end of the quill.

Quill work was not only used on birch bark; in the early years, Indians used quill decorations on their leather clothing. The leather was stretched tight and the quills inserted into it. When it was removed from the frame, the leather naturally tightened, which kept the quills in place. The leather had to be lined with regular leather just as the bark boxes have to be lined to hold the quills in place. A lining was necessary in the clothing to prevent the quills from scratching the wearer.

Most of the decorated quill boxes, like the regular birch-bark baskets and boxes, are fastened together with spruce root and sometimes basswood. Some have extra decorations of sweet grass.

Potato Baskets

Today, most potatos are harvested by machine, but before machines, all potatoes were dug with hand tools by individuals. This chore required strong, sturdy baskets—the type potato baskets the Micmacs and Maliseets have been making for years.

Old ash-splint potato basket. 16" dia, 14" o.h. $15, Maine auction 1986.

New potato basket made by Micmacs. 17" dia, 15" o.h. $30, Vermont basket factory outlet, 1986.

With only a small demand for potato baskets on the farm, but with the increased popularity of baskets of all kinds, new potato baskets are appearing in gift shops and restorations all around New England. They are now enjoying new prestige as wood or magazine baskets. Incidently, they are quite similar to the rice baskets of Louisiana in both shape and size.

Potato Printing

This process is thought to have originated in Massachusetts, or possibly New Hampshire, and is called potato printing because potatoes were so often used to make the designs, or to do the printing. A design was cut into the potato, which was dipped into dye and then pressed onto the basket splints. See Block Printing.

Powaac Roots

Powaac is a root used by Indians to make yellow dye for basket materials. It makes a brilliant shade of yellow.

Ash-splint pumpkin baskets: large, 9½" dia, 7½" h, $95; small, 4½" dia, 3½" h, $25, Maine antique shops, 1986.

Pumpkin-Shaped Baskets

Pumpkin baskets made by the Passamaquoddies (and maybe by other tribes) were not made for harvesting pumpkins, but were made as novelties. They were made to closely resemble pumpkins.

The large pumpkin basket is very realistic with its leaves and sweet-grass stem that doubles as a handle. The small one is adorable because of its size. To make them even more realistic, the ash splints used to make pumpkin baskets were dyed orange with dragon's blood, a powder that could be purchased in stores. Generally, these dyes were made from materials gathered in the forest and fields. In the case of the basket shown here, the Passamaquoddies probably bought the dye in order to get a true orange to represent the true color of a pumpkin. These pumpkin baskets were made during the heydays of the tourist trade, and the basketmakers probably thought the truer orange color would make them sell better.

Pussy Willow

A species of willow used from time to time to make baskets, is the *pussy willow*. It's not as satisfactory as regular willow, but some pussy willow baskets are still being made today. As the willow dries, the weavers shrink, leaving wide spaces in the basket. These can be filled with more weavers, but the baskets are never as satisfactory as those made with regular willow.

Pricing Baskets

Pricing a basket can be difficult, as there are several factors to consider. If a basket is collected with investment in mind, then only perfect examples should be considered. On the other hand, I sometimes will buy a badly damaged basket for study purposes, especially if it is a rare example. Between those extremes are the average collectors who buy baskets because they like and enjoy them, or they want to use them for a particular purpose.

There are also specialized collectors who only collect one type of basketry. They may only collect oak-splint baskets made in their area, or they might only collect one kind of basket, such as porcupine quill boxes. This narrows the field considerably and also affects prices. Scarce items in any field are more expensive than those that are plentiful.

Prices are also affected by locations. For instance, old baskets are much more plentiful in the northeastern part of the country than in other parts. There, ash-splint baskets are especially plentiful and their prices are reasonable compared to other areas. It is not unusual to find as many as two dozen fine-splint baskets in some shops in the area. Ash-splint baskets sell better in the Northeast because collectors are familiar with them. The same applies to cane and pine needle baskets of the Deep South. They are more plentiful there and more reasonably priced.

Quality, workmanship, and condition have a tremendous bearing on price. A basket made by a good basketmaker of quality materials that is still in good condition will always bring top dollar, regardless of the collector or location.

Not surprisingly, New England collectors want baskets made by basketmakers from their area as opposed to baskets from Canada. One of the best ways to distinguish between a basket made in New England and one made in Canada is to look closely at the dyed splints in the bottom. New England basketmakers dyed their splints after they were split, but Canadian makers split theirs after dyeing. The cutting after dyeing leaves a faint white edge on the splints, while the New England-made baskets have solid color splints.

To further confuse the pricing issue, there is the story of two brothers with similar collecting interests. One brother died and his estate sold at auction, in the early 1980s. One of his fine baskets sold for $3,500. The other brother soon found that collecting alone was not as much fun. He was probably thinking about the prices his brother's collection brought, so he decided to sell his own collection at auction. When his baskets sold, the one almost identical to his brother's $3,500 basket sold for just $295. One auction-goer probably summed it up best with his statement, "Antiques from a dead collector always bring more than those from a live collector."

Puccoon Root

Another species of the bloodroot plant used to make an orangey-red dye for basket materials. The puccoon root was used more by basketmakers in the South than in the North.

Early ash-splint and sweet-grass purse, Passamaquoddy. 6" w, 10" l, 7" h. $15, Vermont antique shop, 1986.

Chitimacha cane purse, zipper top, private collection, NPA.

Purses or Handbags

Prior to the 1850s, women had little use for purses or handbags. They raised most of their food and made their own clothing, and if the wife made a large purchase, her husband paid for it. She sold or bartered her eggs, milk, and butter for the few small things she wanted at the store. Most women used little or no makeup and carried no keys or other items found in purses today. They wore aprons with pockets in which they carried snuff boxes or tobacco for their pipes.

Chitamacha envelope-type purse, private collection, NPA.

Ash-splint, sweet-grass and Hong Kong grass purse. 5½" w, 10" l, 7½" h. $19, Maine antique show, 1987.

Factory-made basketry purse with scenes of Westville, Georgia restoration painted around the bottom. 5½" w, 9½" l, 9" h. $10, Georgia flea market, 1986.

Well-decorated ash-splint purse, Unity College colleciton, NPA.

When ready-made purses became available, they were usually ugly little black or brown leather things, called *satchels*. Satchels would be totally unsatisfactory today, and they probably weren't that popular with the ladies of those days, judging by the number of purses they made for themselves—purses of velvet, satin, and other fabrics to match their clothing. Some were encrusted with beads.

By the turn of the century, the purse was an accepted part of milady's outfit, and everybody began making their version of the perfect purse.

During the ensuing years, all kinds of purses were made, but the ones of most interest to basket collectors today are those made of basketry materials—ash splints, sweet grass, and cane, or a combination of these materials.

Basketmakers of the Northeast were probably the first to get into the commercial aspect of basketry purses. They had customers ready to buy—the tourist trade. Southern Indians also made purses, and some of the most beautiful ones were made by the Chitamachas of Louisiana. They made at least two styles, but both were more or less the clutch-style purse. One style had a zipper across the top, while the other was an envelope type.

Purses continued to be made by hand and were hand-decorated. Copies of the Nantucket baskets were made during the forties and fifties in purse form. Also, about that time, a factory-made basketry purse was available to be decorated by people with a flair for painting. Anything could be painted—scenes of the local town, a restoration, or whatever one chose.

Quill Work

Another name for basketry items using porcupine quills. See Porcupine Quill Work.

Rabbit Brush

Indians used the branches of rabbit brush to make finely woven baskets. This plant was given the name *rabbit brush* because its dense growth provides a refuge for the jack rabbits that inhabit areas of the western United States in which the plant grows.

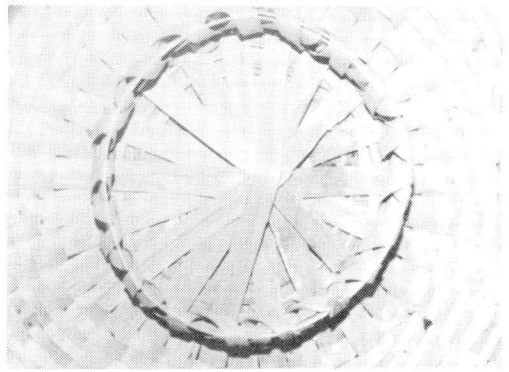

Raised ring inside a feather basket.

Raised Ring Inside Bottom

It's not too unusual to find small baskets with this type woven ring on the outside of the bottom, but it is unusual to find it on the inside.

Raffia

Raffia is the name given to a material obtained from a group of palms that flourish in Madagascar and the surrounding islands. Also spelled *raphia*.

The trees often grow to heights of 75 feet; about 50 feet of it is perfect for making raffia, which is the outer cuticle of the palm. Raffia is a tough, beige-colored material that is cut into strips like thin fabric. It is soft and flexible, easily dyed, and is easy to use. Modern basketmakers—especially Alabama, Louisiana, and Mississippi makers—still use this material. Its durability and adaptability are an asset. Raffia is used to embroider shoes, hats, and purses as well as baskets. Many of the basket books published around the turn of the century suggested that one could use round reeds wrapped in raffia to make an imitation Indian basket.

Fifty years ago, raffia could be bought in at least 25 different colors. Many basketmakers, though, preferred dyeing their own raffia in order to obtain colors that were softer and better suited to what they were making. Dyes that wouldn't work well on other basket materials worked perfectly on raffia. For instance, tea and coffee produced a nice brown, iris petals produced purple, and heather produced a nice yellow. Leaves of the poplar tree produced a different shade of yellow; lily-of-the-valley leaves, and elder and walnut shells produced varying shades of green. Dandelion roots were used to make red dye for raffia.

A Shaker artist could have painted the design on the top and sides of this box, and lined it. 4¾" w, 7¾" l, 2" h. $18, New Hampshire antique mall, fall 1986.

Heart-shaped box with straw doll. 4½" w, 5" l, 2" h. $25, Maine antique shop, fall 1986.

Raffia-Wrapped Grass Boxes

These boxes of unknown origin are often confused with the woven-poplar Shaker boxes. In fact, it is not unusual to find them labeled "Shaker." They're not Shaker. Some have Oriental designs painted on them, and one person reported seeing one with a label from a German candy company. These gift boxes appear to date around the first few decades of the twentieth century.

Although they definitely are not Shaker, one of the brethern of the local Shaker Community (an expert on Shaker history) thought some of the boxes might have been decorated with designs that were handpainted by one of the sisters at the Canterbury, New Hampshire community. He said she was a prolific painter and would paint designs on just about anything. It's very possible she painted floral designs on some of the raffia-wrapped grass boxes to make them more attractive. Also, it is possible that some of the boxes she painted were sold in Shaker stores, provided she could find new boxes to paint. The boxes, however, were not made by the Shakers.

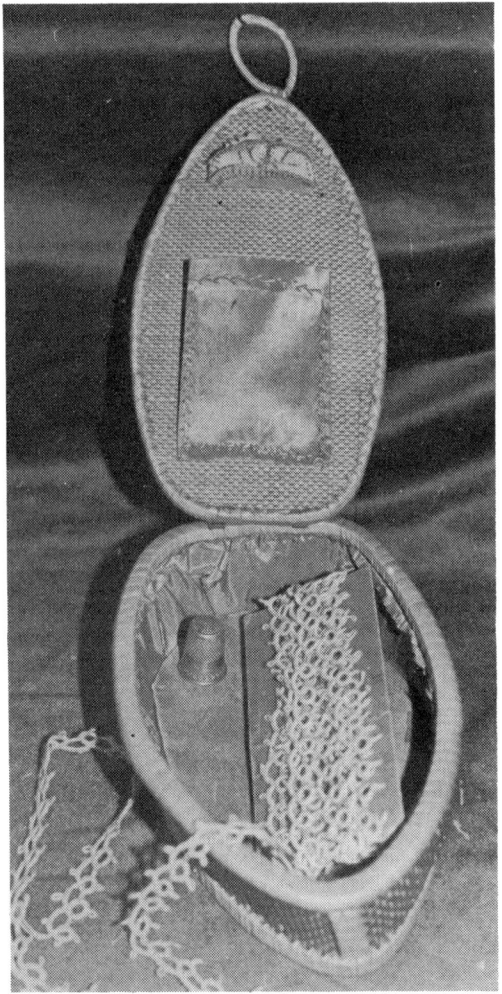

This box was lined by hand to make a sewing box.

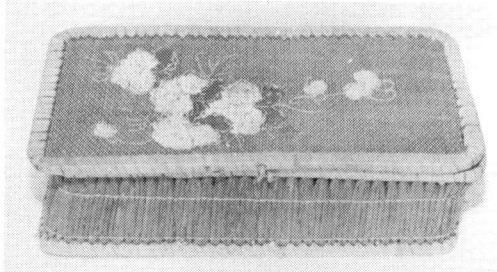

Another style box with design painted on top. 4" w, 9" l, 2" h. $20, New Hampshire antique mall, fall 1986.

One immediately noticeable difference in these gift boxes and those made by Shakers is the type of hinge on the boxes. These boxes have wire hinges whereas the Shaker woven-poplar boxes all had lids fastened on with ribbons—they were always tied. In the early days, sisters of the Shaker community complained about the amount of time required to punch holes with a hand punch. Later, one of the brethern designed and made a punch that could be attached to a table, which was much faster and much easier to use. According to one report, that invention was shared with other Shaker communities where poplar baskets were made.

Rattan

Rattan comes from one of a number of species of climbing palms that have long, round, solid-jointed stems. Rattan can be purchased in round or flat strips and comes in sizes numbering from 1 to 15. This convenience allowed the old basketmakers a wide range of sizes from which to select. It's tough, pliable, and long lasting.

The flat strips were used most often to make seats in chairs. Both the flat and round strips were used in basketry with the majority being used by the later basketmakers who joined the turn of the century revival. Many of makers were urban housewives who found it easier to buy basket materials than to try and go out and gather them. Rural people felt it was a waste of money to buy rattan or any other basketry materials. They continued to go into the woods and fields, as they always had, to get free basket materials.

Rattan sewing basket, private collection, NPA.

Rattan shopping basket, private collection, NPA.

147

Rattan basket, handle missing, 6¾" dia, 6" h. $3, Maine flea market, summer 1986.

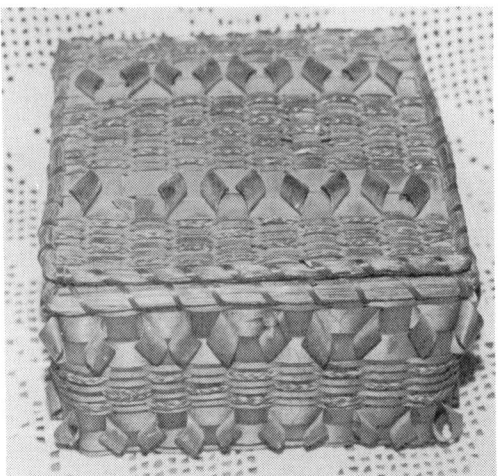

This entire basket is still bright red—dyed, not painted. 6½" square, 4" h. $25, Maine antique shop, 1986.

Red Basket Dye

One of the favorite red dyes of the early settlers, the Cherokee Indians of the Great Smoky Mountains, and the Ozarks was made with *cochineal* (a dye made from the bodies of insects). In New England, much of the red dye was made from berries. One of New England's favorite berries came from a plant called *Solomon's seal* (often called *Nahurmominin* or *eel* berries).

Like the mountaineers and Cherokees, New England makers also used bloodroot to obtain red dye. Another plant of the same family, called *Puccoon,* was used to make an orangey red. Blueberries were used to obtain a reddish pink, but that particular dye didn't have the lasting power of some of the other reds—it faded more quickly. Various solutions had to be used to "set" the colors.

Factory-made red oak-splint basket. 11" w, 17" l, 11" o.h. $17.50, New Hampshire antique mall, fall 1986.

Red Oak Basket

This is a sturdy, factory-made red oak work basket made to be used for carrying small but heavy loads. It appears to be 40 to 50 years old and, at one time, had paper of some kind glued around the top. Remnants of the paper can still be seen.

Reed Sweet Grass

Unlike the sweet vernal grass that grows in pastures and meadows, reed sweet grass grows alongside lakes and streams. In England, it's cut two or three times a year, not only to make grazing land for cattle, but to bale as hay. In the early days of America, reed sweet grass was probably treated the same way, but later it began to be used almost exclusively as basketmaking material. It is believed to be the sweet grass preferred by most basketmakers, and has a sweet fragrance that lingers for years—even when used in basketry.

Ash-splint basket filled with sweet grass ready for basketmaking.

Basket with porcupine decoration and sweetgrass handle and rim, Unity College collection, NPA.

Basket repaired with leather straps, long ago.

Repairing Baskets

Prior to around 1975, baskets were so cheap and the supply so plentiful, nobody looked at damaged baskets unless they wanted one to paint or use for a flower pot. The picture has changed completely. The supply of fine old baskets is dwindling and prices have soared. Now there is more and more talk of repairing baskets.

At auctions and antique shows, sellers will often point out repaired places on the finer baskets. Some of the repair work is so good, it seems rather pointless to mention it. On the other hand, other repair work is obviously made by unskilled repairmen.

Years ago, the finer baskets were repaired although, generally, it was better to make or buy new ones. Even then, some of those repairs were crude.

Sweet grass is probably too difficult to repair, but broken splints can usually be replaced or repaired. Antique dealers specializing in old baskets seldom pass up badly damaged baskets that sell for a few dollars. These baskets can be taken apart and the splints soaked to make them pliable again so they can be reworked into slightly damaged baskets of the same material. With the fine old baskets disappearing into private collections, and prices skyrocketing, it's a safe bet that repairing old baskets will become as popular as wicker repairing.

Rice Baskets

We tend to think of rice as an oriental dish, but Indians were eating it long before the white man arrived. This is especially true of the Indians living in the Great Lakes region of the country, where conditions were not favorable for raising corn. Since they couldn't raise maize, as did other tribes, they depended on the semiaquatic plants growing wild along the edges of the lakes and in the backwaters of the rivers. It is not known what the Indians called wild rice at that time, but the early settlers called it wild oats and wild wheat.

They didn't have to plant or tend wild rice; nevertheless, harvesting and preparing could be an arduous task, beginning with guarding the wild crops from the birds. To keep birds from eating it, the women and girls would tie several stalks of the rice together with basswood twine. When it had matured, the rice was cut and carried home in birch bark canoes. Upon arriving home, the rice had to be hulled, dried, and smoked.

It's not known if the early Indians made a special basket just for rice, but they probably did. When the Cajuns (French Canadians) moved to Louisiana, they not only began growing rice, they made baskets for gathering it. Today, rice is grown commercially and harvested by machines. The rice basket—like so many other harvesting and storage baskets—is no longer needed, but the desire to collect them lingers on.

In Louisiana, the owner described this illustration as an old rice basket without a handle, that was carried under the arm

Old splint and cane rice basket. 16" dia, 10" h. $40, Louisiana antique shop, 1986.

while the worker gathered rice. Holding the basket under the arm while using it has given this rice basket a decidedly warped appearance. Strangely enough, this basket is made of two materials seldom seen in one basket—hickory splints and swamp cane. The spokes are made of splints; the weavers are made of cane.

Rice baskets are similar to Maine potato baskets, but the latter has a handle. The spokes and weavers are also wider and thicker, as they must carry more weight.

Rice Grass

Little information could be found on this type of grass that was supposedly used in early basketry. Oldtime basketmakers say it was an excellent, tough grass for use in coiled basketry. *Rice grass* was probably the name used locally, or it could refer to rice stalks that were used once the grains of rice were removed.

Riddle

A *riddle* is a coarsely woven sieve primarily thought of as being used to separate chaff from grain. This is not necessarily true, as some riddles were used in foundries and mines for sifting coal. There can be no doubt that the one pictured here was used in either a foundry or a mine, as it is covered with thick, black dust that could only come from years of exposure to coal.

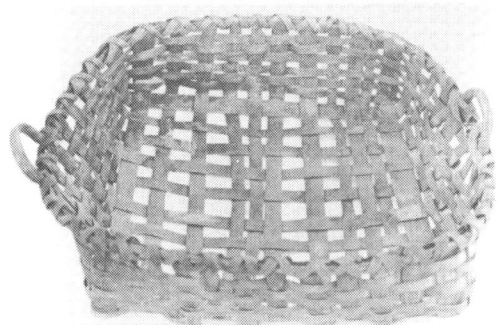

Old splint riddle. 18" square, 5" h. $55, Maine antique show, 1987.

Braided twine or rope basket. 5" dia, 6½" h. $10, Alabama flea market, 1986.

Ring handle on side of ash-splint basket.

Ring Handle

The ring handle is exactly what the name implies—a fancy ring made of the same material as that used in the basket. Generally ring handles are made more for appearance than for service. They are found on the sides of baskets and are used as fasteners for lids.

Rope Basket

Tough Manila rope was made of Manila hemp, and was used by farmers, cattlemen, and others. The hemp was made from the leafstalk of a tree grown in the Philippines, one related to the banana palm. At one time, hemp was used to make paper. Still later, someone invented a rope-twisting or braiding machine. The rope was not tightly twisted, but it was a boon for farmers who could now make cheap, but usable, rope. It appears that someone braided the hemp, then sewed it together to make the basket shown in the illustration.

Rope Handles

Rope handles were not made of rope per se: The rope handle described by basket-making instructors was made by wrapping a long, fine weaver around a thin, round foundation rod. This made it look like a rope; hence, the name *rope handle*. The weavers could be wrapped solidly or widely spaced in sections, or even in three or four coils together at intervals the length of the handle.

Solidly wrapped rope handle.

Rye basket, 10" dia, 8" h, $5, New Hampshire antique shop, 1986.

Rush

Rush includes any plant of the genus *Juncus*. Rush plants include many which are found in low, marshy areas. Cattail and flag are often lumped under this title. In the Northern Hemisphere, some rush plants are tall and slender without leaves, while others have broad leaves. The stalks are used for making mats and baskets, and for caning chairs. A softer species of rush was grown in Japan and used exclusively for making mats.

Rush, like cattail, can be split and dyed to make baskets. Rush should be gathered when it reaches full growth and while the stalk is still green. Old basketmakers knew the rush was ready for cutting when the tips of the leaves began turning brown. In most areas, this occurs around the middle of August. To prepare it for basketmaking, the rush was cut and tied in loose bundles, and then thoroughly dried, either in the shade or in a dark room.

Rye Baskets

Coiled rye baskets are more easily found north of the border states of Tennessee and Kentucky. They can still be found in rather plentiful supplies in Pennsylvania where they are believed to have originated. If old coiled rye baskets are not available, there are plenty of new ones. Old ones were made and used in New England and are fairly plentiful in that area today, along with some new ones. Some are small, delicately made rye baskets, while others are found with coils an inch thick. Rye baskets are still not as popular, nor as expensive, as splint baskets. Generally, they will be found priced from $25 to $125, depending on size, workmanship, and condition. As with all antiques, you can sometimes find a bargain. My bargain is shown in the picture above.

Sabbathday Lake Shaker Trademark

Not all Shaker-made poplar items have trademarks, but it's believed that most of those made at the Sabbathday Lake community in Maine were stamped with this trademark. It's even possible that all woven poplar items were made at Shaker communities—since freezing temperatures are necessary to cure the wood, it's doubtful that woven poplar items were made in the South. Probably New Hampshire, New York, and Maine are the only places where Shaker-made poplar items were made.

Trademark found on the bottom of Sabbathday Lake woven-poplar boxes.

Sandstone

Sandstone is a coarse-grained rock used mostly in building—usually flagstone walks and patios. It's also used for whetstones and grindstones, but it's most important use for basketmakers is as a fine-grained sandstone for smoothing basket materials. The Hopi used it extensively as did some other tribes.

Ash-splint and sweet-grass sandwich basket, Unity College collection, NPA.

Sandwich Basket

The same basket that was used for cakes could be used for sandwiches. Like the uncovered cake basket, the sandwich basket was kept in the home and used to serve sandwiches on the veranda, or in the gazebo.

Sassafras

The small tree that supplied sassafras tea for our ancestors also furnished bark to use in basketmaking. *Sassafras,* any of a number of related trees of the *laurel* family, is easily identified by its yellow flowers and bluish fruit. The dried roots of the sassafras are used for both medicine and flavoring. Its reddish-brown bark is tough enough for spokes and can be split to make weavers.

Seal Gut

Seal gut was traditionally used by the Alaskan basketmakers to add fancy designs on baskets. See Yupik Eskimo Baskets.

Sedge

Sedge grows throughout the United States. One species seems to thrive in the sandy lands of the southern part of the country. Both the Indians and whites have long praised it as a multipurpose basketry material. It can be used to make yellow dye; the long, tough, woody interior of the roots is used to make white designs on coiled baskets. The flexible grass stems can be used for coiling.

Seminole Indians

The Muskhogean family of Indians, of which the Seminoles are members, was one of the great Indian families of the South. Before the arrival of the later southern aristocracy, these were the Indian aristocrats of the South. Alabama, Georgia, Mississippi, and parts of Tennessee were considered their territory until the white man came.

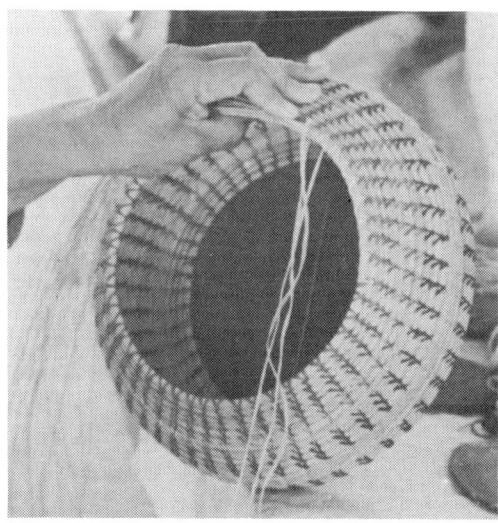

Coiling a grass basket.

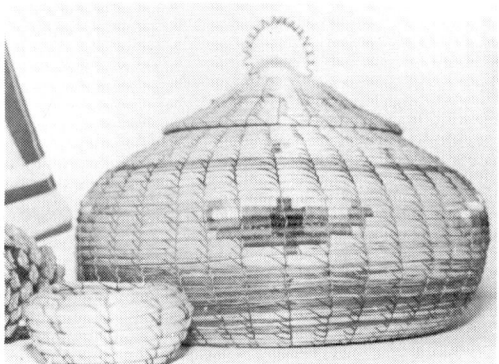

Completed pine needle basket. 10" dia, 8" h. $90, Indian reservation, 1986.

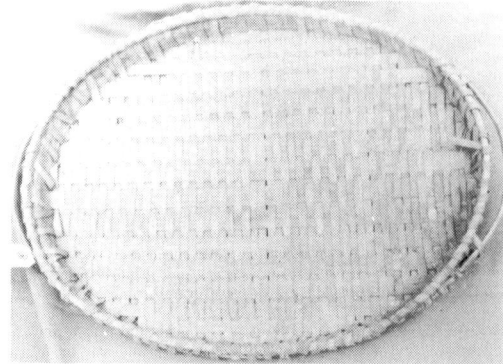

Large oak-splint serving tray. 15" w, 20" l. $150, Tennessee auction, 1986.

Oak-splint tray with a reinforced strip through the center. 14" w, 23" l. $150, Tennessee auction, 1986.

At first, the Muskhogean moved to Florida because it was owned by the Spanish and they thought it would be safe. Florida was then sold to the United States, and after many battles and skirmishes, some of the Seminoles agreed to go to Oklahoma. Those who didn't agree (there were quite a few), instead fled to the Everglades where they are today.

The Seminoles, like the Miccosukees, make baskets of coiled pine needles sewn together with waxed thread. They also make a frame of bark or cypress over which they arrange their hair to achieve a hat-brim effect.

Serving Tray

Among the many things that can be made of woven oak splints, is the serving tray, and basketmakers take great pride in their handiwork when making these trays. While other types are less expensive, handmade serving trays are often preferred. Serving trays were especially popular as late as the 1950s when there was quite a bit of entertaining in the home. The basketry tray was handy for serving anything from hors d'oeuvres at a party to lemonade on the porch. Serving trays have been made of most basketry materials, including rattan and splints. Some later versions were made of pine needles with sea shell scenes beneath their glass-covered bottoms. These were made primarily for the tourist trade.

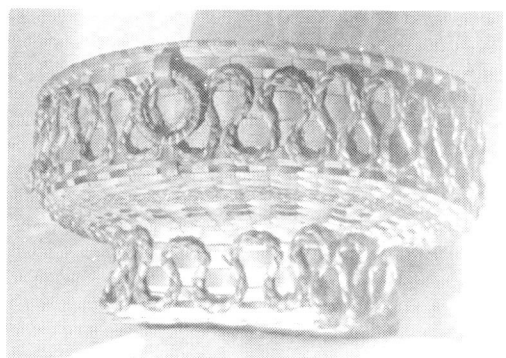

Ash-splint and sweet-grass sewing basket attributed to the Passamaquoddies. 9½" dia, 5" h. $35, Maine antique auction, 1986.

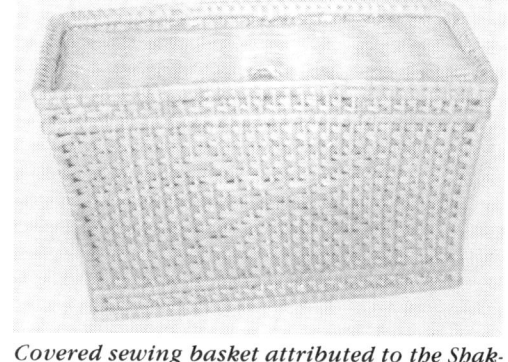

Covered sewing basket attributed to the Shakers. 5¼" w, 9¾" l, 5½" h. $45, Maine antique show, 1987.

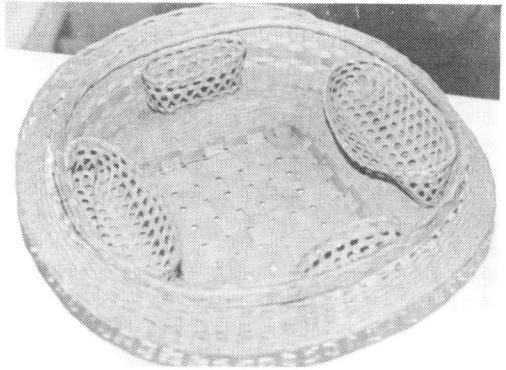

The inside of a sewing basket, showing the pockets.

Inside of sewing basket, showing pockets.

Sewing basket of ash splints turned to look like flower petals, Unity College collection, NPA.

Sewing Basket

If one were to take a survey on the subject, chances are, the results would show that sewing baskets were made in a wider variety of shapes, styles, and materials than any other type of basketry item.

There were open sewing baskets and closed sewing baskets, as well as those in round, square, and oblong shapes. Some had handles; others didn't. Some were made plain, while others were fitted with places for needles, thread, pincushions, and scissors.

Sewing baskets were popular because everyone needed at least one, sometimes two. Often, a girl was as young as five years old when she began learning "her stitches," and she, too, needed a sewing basket.

Three-finger, wooden Shaker sewing basket lined with satin and fitted with satin pincushion and woven poplar needle case; has Sabbathday Lake trademark. 12" l, 7½" w, 10" o.h.. $125, Maine auction, 1987.

Today, old sewing baskets are quite collectible. Some are still used as they were originally intended, while others are used for other purposes. Some are perfect for dried-flower arrangements, and some of the old willow sewing baskets make great fruit baskets. One young girl uses several different kinds of covered sewing baskets to hold her costume jewelry.

Prior to the invention of the sewing machine in the 1800s, all clothing and household linens were made by hand. Sewing baskets were essential and were used frequently, almost daily. The ladies were as involved in mending old things as they were in making new ones.

The very first "sewing baskets" were simply conventional baskets used to hold sewing items. They were made of whatever materials were available in the area—oak splints, hickory splints, pine needles, cane, and vines in the South; ash splints, sweet grass, willow, birch bark, and reed in the North. In the Southwest, basketmakers used willow, yucca, and whatever other grasses were available.

After the basketry revival around the turn of the century (when instruction books on basketry began to come into publication), reed and raffia were suggested as the best and easiest materials to find and use for making baskets. It was also at about this time that bamboo sewing baskets began to be imported in large numbers.

Covered ash-splint sewing stand. 13" dia, 24" h. $55, Maine antique show, 1987.

Sewing Stands

Sewing and mending were most important in the early days of this country, so both sewing baskets and sewing stands were made. Stands, like the baskets, were made of many materials and in many styles. In many cases, they are woven of the same materials. Some are now classified as wicker,

Ash-splint sewing stand with round containers, Unity College collection, NPA.

Ash-splint sewing stand with square containers. 12" square, 29" h. $50, damaged, Maine antique shop, 1986.

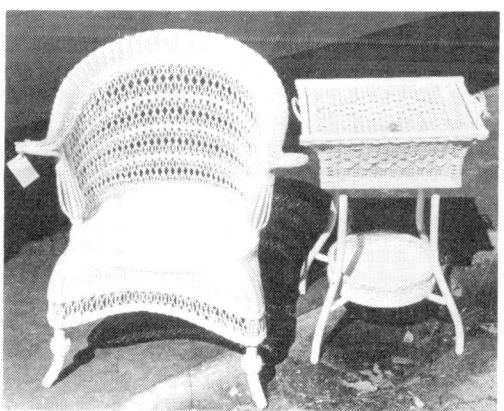

Wicker sewing stand with wicker chair, private collection, NPA.

but since there is actually only a slight difference between the two, they can be classified and used together. Some were made during the Roaring Twenties. What is now called *wicker* furniture was, at that time, called *basket furniture*.

Beautiful sewing stands were made by basketmakers in the Northeast. The legs were usually made of hardwood, while the two containers were made of ash splints. Most of these have the decorative looping found on other ash-splint baskets. Some of the stands are open; others are covered.

Reproduction Shaker basket bought at a Shaker store, described as a cat's head with a band of onion-skin dye. 9½" dia, 12" o.h. $36, Shaker store, 1985.

Shaker Baskets

Today, with the growing interest in anything Shaker, it's not unusual to see ordinary baskets labeled or described as *Shaker* or Shaker-type. In an attempt to educate the public, much has been written about Shaker baskets. Several collectors have pointed out how easy it is to mistake the Bushwhacker or Taconic baskets with those made by the Shakers, and vice versa.

The Shakers made and sold thousands of baskets in their community stores scattered throughout New England, Kentucky, and Ohio. They also sold thousands of baskets they bought from individual basketmakers who made them to Shaker specifications. The average basketmaker made the complete basket from start to finish, but the Shakers worked on a production line of sorts, or maybe it should be called a community effort. A completed basket was not an individual accomplishment; instead, each person did the job for which he or she was best qualified or trained.

The Shakers were organized by Mother Ann Lee. They arrived in North America, from England, in 1774. Shortly thereafter, they began making ash-splint baskets, a craft they are believed to have learned from the Indians.

The Shakers were an industrious and ingenious people, so they were soon designing and making their own styles of baskets. It is not known when the Shakers first became interested in commercial ventures, but by 1816 they had established a reputation for excellent workmanship and quality, and the demand for their handmade items had increased to the point at which they had to open stores in most of their communities. The Shakers sold their handmade items in the stores and later established routes through which they sold them.

Sometime after 1850, demand shifted from the larger utilitarian baskets to smaller, fancier baskets—the type that appealed to "summer people" (people spent their summers in the nearby resorts). As the demand grew, the Shaker community streamlined its operation: In order to speed up the supply, each person was assigned the job he or she was most qualified to do.

Basketmaking continued at the Shaker communities for several decades; then, as the number of residents in the communities (they were a celibate order) began to decline, and the demand for baskets lessened, they made fewer and fewer baskets.

One, among the various styles of baskets made by the Shakers, was the *Cat's Head*—so named because the bottom of it resembled a cat's head. A smaller version was called a *Kitten's Head*. Other styles were the *spoon basket,* a miniature basket with cupped sides that resembled a spoon; a hexagon-weave cheese basket; a set of nesting baskets that vaguely resembled the Nantucket Lightship baskets; a so-called *Deaconess* basket that was actually a well-made oblong basket, similar to some market baskets; fruit and apple baskets; and perhaps the most interesting of all, the baskets made to hold wood chips for the stoves. A wood-chip basket was placed in each room of the house. The most intriguing feature of the wood-chip basket was the pair of wooden strips attached along each side of the bottom of the basket so that it could "skate" along on snowy pathways rather than have to be carried by the handle. Also taken into account when the basket was designed, was how heavy it would be when filled with wood chips, so handles were attached to both ends of the oblong basket.

Most baskets made by the Shakers had stationary handles; few, if any, had swing handles.

Large Shaker woven-poplar box. 10" square, 3¼" h. $175, damaged, New Hampshire antique shop, 1986.

Shaker woven-poplar box, different design. 3½" square, 2" h. $100, Shaker store, 1986.

Inside of smaller box, pink satin lining. 6¼" square, 2¼" h. $125, Shaker store, 1986.

Shaker Boxes

Since the dictionary defines a basket as a container made of interwoven twigs and rushes, thin strips of wood, and other flexible materials, the beautifully woven-poplar boxes made by the Shakers would have to be included in basketry books.

It's easy to appreciate the intricacy of Shaker boxes simply by looking at them, but when collectors learn of the long, tedious work required to make them, their appreciation grows.

Chores around the Shaker communities were given to those best qualified for the job; therefore, the first step in making boxes was to assign the best woodsmen the chore of selecting the finest poplar trees (they would only use trees growing in moist land). Once the trees were cut, they were taken to the sawmill to be cut into lengths of 24 inches—no more, no less. The next step was to remove the bark and cut the lengths of wood into blocks that measured about 2½ square inches.

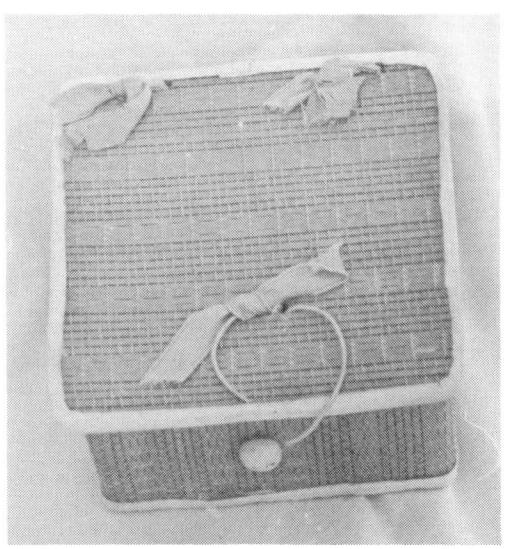

Woven Shaker poplar box. 3½" square, 2" h, $75, Maine antique show, 1986; all boxes have Shaker trademark.

The Shaker men soon discovered that poplar blocks could be cut into much smoother, paper-thin pieces if they were kept frozen, so the wood was stacked outside and even covered with water to assure freezing.

The first chore relegated to the women was culling imperfect strips and then sorting them. Not surprisingly, baskets were used in the basketmaking process—splints were taken by the basketful to the laundry room to be dried.

At first, the number of Shaker boxes to be made was limited to the amount of wood obtained from seventeen logs. But when sales increased and production reached its peak, the Shakers were using three to four cords of wood per year.

Cutting, drying, and sorting weren't the only chores connected with making the boxes—the thin strips of poplar had to be cut into tiny pieces, each one only a fraction of an inch wide. The Shakers began weaving their first poplar boxes in the 1860s, and by 1872 they were still cutting poplar strips by hand; finally, in 1872, one of the brethern designed and built a machine to cut the strips quickly and easily.

After cutting, the next step was to weave the poplar strips together, and for that chore, the Shaker brethern built a special loom—one similar to those used for weaving fabric. The tiny strips were woven together with sewing thread, and the woven material was cut off when it reached a length of approximately ten yards. Then, began the final process of putting the boxes together. The material was ironed between two sheets of white paper to insure that it was thoroughly dry and to make it stronger. Box sizes were already established, so the basketmakers knew exactly what size to cut each piece of material, and pieces of cardboard were cut to match, as the woven poplar needed reinforcement. The linings—velvet for jewelry boxes and satin for others—were glued to one side of the cardboard, and the woven poplar was glued to the other side. The edges were bound with thin strips of white leather, and the top was fastened on with satin ribbons.

In 1899 one of the sisters introduced using a few strands of sweet grass when making a poplar box. Nowhere have records been found indicating that Shaker boxes were made entirely of sweet grass. The woven-poplar boxes with the few strands of sweet grass were made for a few years, but they never gained the popularity of the boxes made entirely of woven poplar. Some believe this was due to the fact that sweet grass was associated with baskets made by the Indians, while the woven poplar was traditionally Shaker.

Sales of poplar boxes reached such proportions, the Shakers eventually published a catalogue picturing, describing, and pricing many of their boxes. When the *Catalogue of Fancy Goods* was published, customers had a choice of 32 items at prices ranging from 25 cents for a tray to $3.25, which would buy several types of boxes. Prices on the same boxes today range from around $75 to $300.

Closed picnic basket attributed to Shakers. 7" w, 13" l, 13" o.h. $75, little damage, Maine antique shop, 1986.

Shaker Picnic Basket

Perhaps there should be a question mark in front of the word *Shaker* in this category. Baskets of this type are on display at the Shaker Museum in Old Chatham, New York, but curator Jan Christman can authenticate neither those nor this one (above photo) as having actually been made by the Shakers. This type was sold in the Shaker stores, but Shakers are known to have bought baskets made by others (but made to their rigid specifications). The basket pictured here may or may not be an authentic Shaker basket. A strange thing about this one is the paper lining. Whether it was placed there originally and meant to be removed later, or was added later to protect the inside, is unknown.

Shaving Horse

The *shaving horse,* used to split and smooth ash splints, very much resembles the harness maker's horse—the upright wooden contraption used to hold leather tautly while it is sewn. Both items shown here were handmade—and probably to the user's specifications. The shaving horse, also called a *drawing horse,* was used to hold poplar and ash splints in order to shave them even thinner, and make them smoother.

Shaving horse, Penobscot Indian Museum, NPA.

Shelf tray of woven, dyed oak splints, private collection, NPA.

Shelf Baskets or Trays

Shallow square and oblong trays were made to be used in presses, cupboards, and armoires. There were no closets as such, and no paper boxes in which to store clothing, so the people used shallow baskets and trays that had lids to keep out dust and rodents.

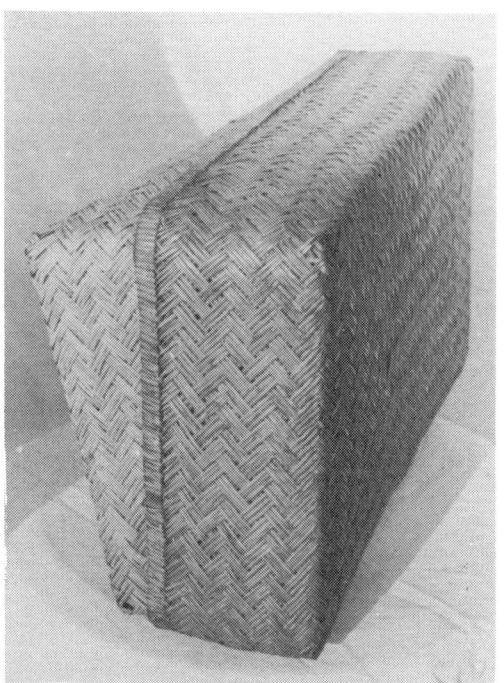

Covered storage basket of a much later period, triple-woven cane. 14" w, 24" l, 7" h. $25, Maine antique show, 1987.

Ash-splint, sweet-grass, and Hong Kong grass shopping bag. 7" w, 14½" l, 16" o.h. $19, Maine antique mall, 1986.

Shopping Bags, Woven

Every basketmaker, worthy of the name, has at one time or another made a bag or basket to be used for general shopping. There seems to have been a tendency among all basketmakers to make deep round or square baskets for grocery shopping, and smaller oblong ones for general shopping.

After marketing, ladies had their afternoons free to go back into town to buy little things they needed, such as small pieces of lace and ribbon, or embroidery threads. A small basket was fine for this type of shopping. Later on, purchases were wrapped in paper and tied with a string, but they would have been difficult to carry without a shopping basket.

Ash-splint shopping basket, Passamaquoddy. 5½" w, 16" l, 18" o.h. $35, Vermont antique shop, summer 1986.

Sifter

When and where this sifter was made is unknown, but the workmanship is absolutely superb. Unlike most sifters that have splints fastened around the bottom, this one has them fastened into points on the sides. It may have been used for winnowing grain or rice, but more than likely it was used to sift meal before making cornbread. Other sifters were made plain with a splint bottom.

Fancy sifter with splints fastened on the sides. 18" dia, 4½" h. $125, Main auction, 1987.

Plain sifter with pine band. 16" dia, 4½" h. $55, Rhode Island antique shop, 1986.

Singe

It's nearly impossible to remove all of the superficial hair-like threads on baskets made from oak, hickory, and elm splints, unless the hairs are singed lightly. If they're singed for too long, or too much, the fire will, of course, burn the splints. A light singeing will remove all the stray hairs or threads.

Single-Wrapped Rims

Concern about the wrapping on the top and rim of a basket is limited almost exclusively to splint baskets. A coil basket doesn't have that type of rim, but it does have to be secured well, as do all baskets.

Basket with single-wrapped rim and notched handle.

Single-wrapped is not as strong or as sturdy as double-wrapped and may not last as long. Single-wrapped means the splint was wrapped around the rim once and no more.

Skep

Another name for beehives made of coiled rye grass. See Beehives.

Skunk

Indians have always used the materials available to them and have copied things familiar to them—things they see daily. In the bayou country of southern Louisiana, the Coushattas took pine needles and black and white raffia to fashion a very realistic skunk basket. The lid fits the small opening on top, making this a useful basketry container.

Pine needle effigy of a skunk. 2¾" dia, 5½" l including tail. $20, Coushatta reservation, 1986.

Smilax

Smilax has long been a favorite vine for decorations, especially at Southern weddings. Smilax has also been used to make baskets. When the roughness is removed from the vines, they make strong, flexible spokes and weavers for baskets.

Soloman's Seal

The berries of this plant (polygonatum biflorum) were used by the New England basketmakers to make red dye for their basket materials. It's one of the perennial plants with bell-shaped flowers and dark red berries. The name is believed to come from the markings on the roots. See Red Dye.

Sotol

Any number of related tree-like plants growing in the deserts of the Southwest. They also grow in northern Mexico. The plant has clusters of whitish, lilylike flowers and leaves that can be split into small quarter-inch strips and used in making twilled baskets. Sharp, thorny teeth-like growths on the leaves have to be removed before they can be used.

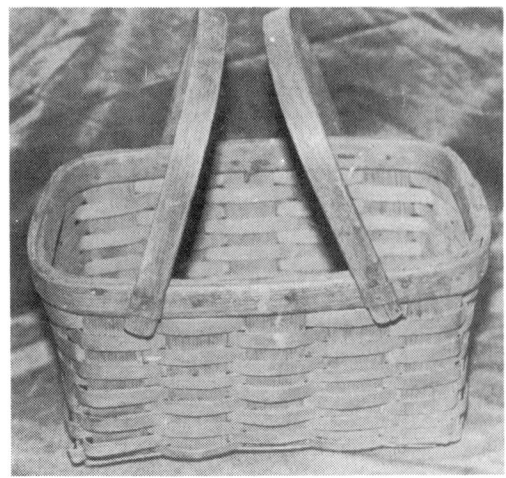

In some areas, oak-splint baskets like this were used for sowing. 7" w, 12" l, 11" o.h. $25, Maine auction, 1986.

Sowing Baskets

There were sowing baskets just as there were sewing baskets. The latter was used in the house to keep sewing needs while the former might be fastened around the waist, draped over the shoulder, or carried in the hand. The sowing basket was filled with seeds that could be dropped in hills or broadcast over fields.

Spokes

Spokes are the splints used to form the bottom of a woven basket; they're continued up to where the sides of the basket will be, forming a foundation for later weaving. Spokes have to be strong if the basket is going to be sturdy and durable. In most baskets, the spokes are a bit heavier than the splints used as weavers. Also called *standards*.

Spruce Roots

In early writings, this tree was referred to as *spruse*, and even then the use of spruce roots for sewing baskets together, especially birch-bark baskets and boxes, was discussed. In fact, spruce roots are as important to some basketmakers as oak splints are to others.

Sitka spruce, grown in areas of Alaska and California, was very important to basketmakers who boiled the roots, then split them to make a coarse foundation splint. Black, white, and red spruce grow best in the northern part of the country, and all three have tough, flexible roots that are excellent for use in basketry. Spruce roots were almost indispensable for making birch-bark containers; they were needed to sew the boxes together. Small roots, excellent for sewing small birch-bark pieces, could usually be found around the younger trees, but if it was not available, the worker could peel and scrape the roots down to the needed size. It also could be split for finer sewing.

Square Bottom/Round Top

Basketmakers used to say that making a basket with a square bottom and a round top required lots of skill. But making this bonnet basket shouldn't have been that difficult; the maker put a solid wooden rim around the top, forcing it into the desired size and shape.

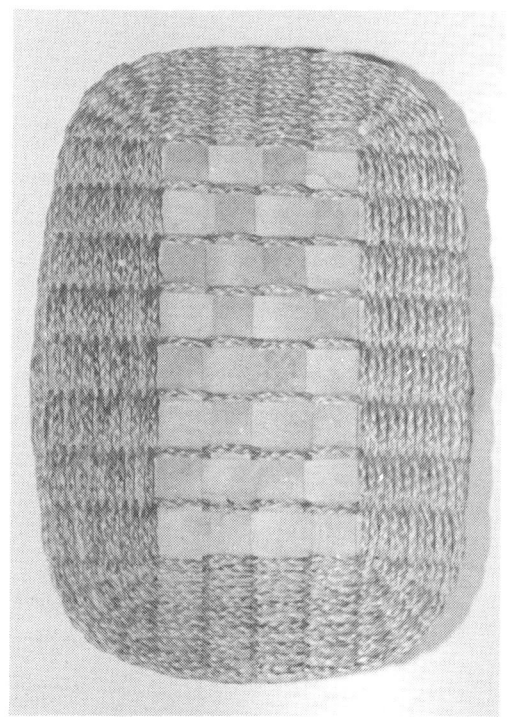

Ash-splint and sweet-grass stationery basket, Unity College collection, NPA.

Rim of square basket showing how the round top was made.

Squaw Grass

Squaw grass is another name for Golden Ragwort. It grows all over America, mostly in moist meadows and swamps, and is used in basketry. See Golden Ragwort.

Stationery Basket

It has been said that when the Indians of Maine discovered tourists, they found them to be one of their best natural resources. For a century or more, tourists flocked to Maine to spend their summers. As was the vacationing custom in those days, the entire family spent the summer at a spa or favorite resort hotel, usually on the coast. Not only did they have the entire coast, they had places like Bar Harbor, Old Orchard, and Poland Spring. Families came bringing their maids, governesses, and coachmen. Horse and carriage arrived on the same train as the family and servants, and quarters were provided for both servants and horses.

It didn't take long for the basketmakers—whites, Indians, and Shakers—to discover the lucrative tourist market. Before, basketmakers made mostly utilitarian baskets, but suddenly, they began making what they previously would have considered to be frivolous—things like stationery baskets.

The tourists of that day were a letter-writing crowd—people wrote their friends rather than call them on the telephone. Correspondence was heavy and postage was only a penny for a postcard and two cents for a letter. A stationery basket was very handy for holding incoming and outgoing mail.

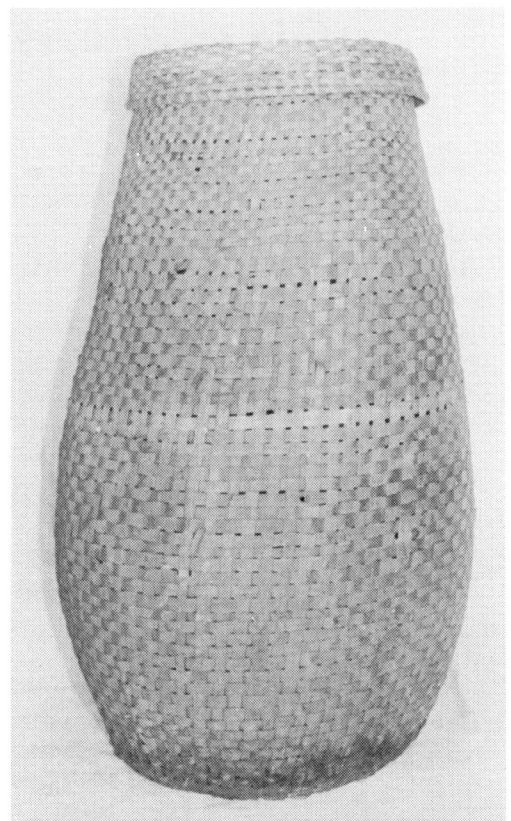

Plain ash-splint storage basket. 14" dia, 30" h. $125, Vermont antique mall, 1987.

Stitched grass basket. 6" dia, 3" h, 9" o.h. $5, Maine estate sale, 1986.

Stitched Grass Basket

It is not known when or where these stitched grass baskets were made. They're not very attractive, and apparently, few were made. Not many are seen now. The stitched grass basket shown in the illustration here is an unusual one. The lid was made to fit over the handle and cannot be removed; it can only raised and lowered.

Storage or Utility Baskets

Ask a dozen oldtimers how storage baskets were used, and you'll probably get a dozen different answers. Apparently, they were used for whatever the owner needed them for at the moment. Some say they were used as feather baskets; others say they were used to store feather beds in the summer when it was too hot to sleep on them. No doubt, they were also used for clothing storage and possibly for household linens.

Notice how fragile-looking the handles are, especially for use on something as large as a storage basket. The plain storage basket doesn't even have handles.

Fancy ash-splint storage basket with dyed, but badly faded weavers. 19" dia, 28" h. $115, Maine antique show, 1986.

Open Cherokee-made cane storage basket, private collection, NPA.

Strawberry-picking basket with two factory-made quart size containers. 26" l, 11½" o.h. $10, Maine antique shop, 1986.

Strawberry-Picking Baskets

This is a primitive strawberry-picking basket and is used here to complete the basketry picture. The wooden carrier was handmade—not woven, coiled, or twined—and it was built to hold eight factory-made quart baskets (the poorly made dispensable type that could be filled with berries and then sold without changing the berries from one container to another). In many strawberry-growing areas, strawberry-picking baskets are being phased out and are slowly finding their way into antique shops, shows, and malls.

Strawberry-Shaped Basket

The Passamaquoddy Indians of Maine were the first to make the various baskets shaped like fruits and nuts. Using ash splints and red dye, they concocted a strawberry-shaped basket similar to the acorn basket. It's shaped like a strawberry with red curliques around the side and green leaves on the top for a very realistic look.

Straw and Skin Dryer

The only feature of this contraption that would remotely connect it with basketry is the coiled straw sides. This is truly basketry in its most primitive form. Origin and use are unknown, but the dealer who sold it thought it might have been used for drying something like seed or wool. The outside is made of sheep skin, and some primitively cured, small pieces of wool are still attached. Five coils of wrapped straw were placed inside to keep the bottom taut and the sides standing; otherwise, it would collapse.

Straw and skin dryer. 15" dia, 3½" h. $30, New England antique show, 1987.

String Holder

The majority of old string holders were made of either wood or iron, but there were a few made of basketry materials. Some were made to resemble beehives—flat on the bottom and rounded at the top, with a hole in the top for thread to come through. Later string holders were made of rattan on a plywood base. The wood and iron string holders were mostly used in grocery and department stores; before the introduction of paper and plastic bags, string was needed to wrap packages. A large number of ash-splint and sweet-grass string holders were made in the Northeast and sold to tourists for use in the home.

Sumac

Sumac was one of the most useful plants in basketmaking with the exception of various splints and pine needles. The stalk was used in making basket foundations, and also yellow dye was obtained from it. The slender branches of the low-growing sumac were used by Indians more than any other rod material, except for willow. By simply putting the peeled sumac branches in water filled with berry stems from the alder, the branches were easily dyed to make dark weavers. Sumac is a versatile plant: The powdered leaves from some species are used for tanning and dyes, while other species are used in medicine.

Sumitori Kago

Sumitori kago is the Japanese name for the basket that was used for holding brazier charcoal in homes. In earlier days, a *brazier* was used to heat each room of the house, and a container was necessary to keep a supply of charcoal on hand. Although these baskets were not often seen, the workmanship on the sumitori kago was as excellent as that on the finest basket.

Sweet Vernal Grass

Sweet vernal grass is the correct name, but in many places it is called *sweet grass* by those who use it in basketry. Growing abundantly in both England and the eastern part of the United States, it is a sweet-scented grass that gives the surrounding area a marvelous, light-scented fragrance—hence, its name. The fragrance of sweet grass lingers for years after it's woven or coiled into baskets.

Much sweet grass was used in the Passama-quoddy-made baskets.

Sweetzer Baskets

The Sweetzer family has been making baskets in Waterbury, Vermont, for more than 125 years. Unlike so many old basketmaking families today, the fourth generation of this family continues to make the same type baskets as those of their earlier generations, and they still use ash splints.

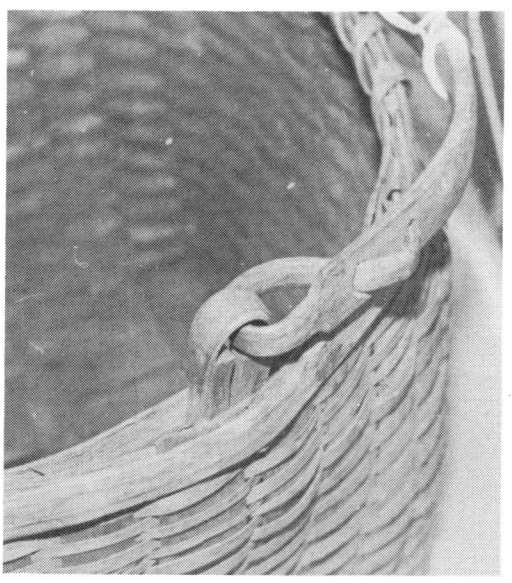

Desirable swing-handle basket, self-fastened.

Hairpin-loop, fastened swing-handle basket.

Poor replica of the Nantucket basket; the swing-handle is fastened with brass screws.

Old basket with crudely attached swing-handle.

Swing-Handle Baskets

Swing-handle baskets, are the most sought-after of the old woven-splint baskets. Basketmakers have always made swing-handles—usually on burden or work baskets—and through the years, many of the handles have simply worn out. It's difficult to attribute swing-handles—or as they are sometimes called, *drop handles*—to any one maker, with the exception of the Taghkanic or Bushwhacker baskets, the Nantucket Lightship basket, and the new ones being made today. Many of the skilled basketmakers today are making swing-handles because they're more sought after and higher priced. It is not unusual to find new, well-made swing-handles priced in the $500-and-up bracket.

169

A swing-handle basket is classified as such when the handle is free swinging; that is, it will fall to either side, allowing the basket to be filled without interference from the handle (but the handle can be raised when needed).

Not all swing-handles were beautifully made. Some were simply bolted onto a wooden splint or ear that rose above the top of the basket. There are all kinds of swing-handle baskets, but the most expensive and sought-after is the kind having a loop or hole at the end of the handle, that fits into a loop or hole made at the top of the basket.

Taconic Baskets

Also known as Bushwhacker baskets. Made for well over a century by a group living in the New York village of Taghkanic, now simplified to Taconic. See Bushwhacker Baskets.

Crudely cut splints, what appears to be some kind of cord weavers, and a tall, vine handle make up this basket. 6" square, 18" o.h. $10, Maine antique show, 1986.

Tall-Handled Baskets

Making baskets in the eras of long ago was a task somewhat like an experienced cook experimenting with various dishes. The cook wanted to try something new—maybe a new combination. Basketmakers did the same thing: They made whatever they liked, wanted, or needed. No explanation has been found as to why basketmakers made such tall handles on some of the baskets.

Tall-handled ash-splint basket. 4½" w, 9½" l, 21" o.h. $15, Maine antique show, fall 1986.

170

Tamarack

Also known as *tamarack pine,* it is found along the Pacific coast, from California to Alaska. Other species are found in swamps and cooler places. Tamarack roots were used by some of the older Indians in their basketry.

Small Tarahumara basket of palm fiber. 2½" dia, 4" h. $10, Indian reservation, 1986.

Tarahumara Indians

By the boundries established today, the Tarahumaras would be considered Mexican Indians; however, in the early days, they ignored boundries—except when the boundaries concerned another's hunting grounds.

The area inhabited by the Tarahumaras was a rugged, arrid area that didn't encourage agriculture. For that reason, they developed a lifestyle much like the early basketmakers—a simple lifestyle that was mostly self-sufficient. Living this somewhat isolated existence in the mountainous country of northern Mexico, the Tarahumaras experienced many hardships through the years, and were faced with poverty and near starvation at times.

Only recently have they acquired plastic containers to replace the baskets they made and used throughout the centuries. They had long been making lidded baskets, called *piticas*, which were usually made of twilled bear grass. Like so many others at that time, they used baskets to store their possessions.

There was a time when every Tarahumara woman made baskets, but today it's difficult to find many of the beautiful, double-woven, lidded piticas. They still make a few single-weave baskets, but most of them are only one to four inches tall.

Fancy ash-splint and cord tatting basket. 4½" dia, 5½" h. $17, Alabama antique shop, 1986.

Tatting Basket

Tatting was fancy stitchery work enjoyed by many ladies over the years. It was tedious work, but the ladies could take it with them when visiting neighbors or traveling by train, or they could tat as they sat around on the porches of resort hotels during the summer. Nearly every lady did some sort of fancy needlework in those days—it was like the badge of a good homemaker. Naturally, the ladies were delighted with the small tatting baskets they could carry on their arms—baskets that would hold their tatting shuttle and thread.

Lined basket with Rose Medallion teapot. 7" w, 10" l, 6½" h. $125, Massachusetts antique shop, 1987.

Teapot Basket

There is hardly a home in New England that doesn't have a treasure trove of gifts brought from around the world. For centuries, men have sailed the seas and brought back gifts for family and friends. Baskets like the one in the illustration here were brought back (and many were imported) to use during tea time. This basket contained a Rose Medallion teapot and was lined to protect it. The basket is made of reeds wrapped with what appears to be thinly cut bamboo. The handle and fasteners are brass. Some of the baskets also contain cups to match the teapot.

Thompson River Indians

The name was derived from their location, the Thompson River, in Canada. Also called Thompson Indians. They were noted for their excellent baskets made with bold geometric designs.

Tobacco Baskets

In places like Tennessee and Kentucky, where tobacco is grown, cut, dried, and then carried to the tobacco auctions, farmers use a flat basket contraption that more closely resembles the lid from a large basket than anything else. Called simply a *tobacco basket,* this type of basket is beginning to show up in antique shops around the country. It is large, approximately 40 × 40 square inches, and factory-made using loosely woven 6-inch splints. Some antique dealers say there is now a big demand for these baskets among younger people who use them for wall decorations. More surprising than their popularity are the prices they're bringing. In New England, the going price is $33–$55 each.

Tufted Hair Grass

This is one of the many grasses used in basketry. It is most likely found in one of three places: rich soil in drained fields, clay woodlands, and on the banks of rivers and streams. When sheltered by trees, it becomes very luxuriant. Tufted hair grass has strong, stiff stems that grow as high as two and three feet. It grows extremely well in the mountains of New Mexico, and in California where the split stems are used to make a white design in split-root baskets.

Tule

Tule can best be described as a kind of large bullrush. It is found in marshy places in the West and Southwest and is used extensively in basketry. In fact, tule can be used in a number of ways. The slender roots of the plant can be dried and used for twining a red design in weaving, and the stems can be split or left whole for use in large baskets. The section between the roots and stem is the most valuable of all: The bark can be split from this section and used to make mats, and the outside of the stems can be split into very narrow strips, then twisted into thin threads for use in making twined baskets.

Tumpline

A *tumpline* was a carrying strap fastened on a basket, then put across the carrier's head in order to carry heavy burden baskets. Some tribes made skull-cap type hats to protect their heads against the weight of tumplines. Since many Indian families moved frequently during those early years, it was necessary to move their food and, in some cases, their lodging. They had no other means of transporting their possessions than by canoe, sled, or basket and tumpline. By using a tumpline, a man or woman could carry from 100 to 150 pounds with ease.

Turtle

Using their skills and experience, the Coushatta made the effigy of a turtle. Using pine needles and raffia, they created a small turtle-shaped container that is unbelievably realistic looking. Like the other animals they make, the turtle has a cover over the storage compartment on its back. Actually, it makes a quite safe jewelry box, as few thieves would expect to find jewelry in a pine needle container shaped like a turtle.

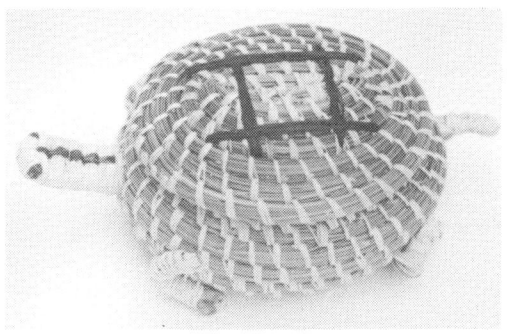

Pine needle and raffia turtle. 2¾" w, 4½" l, 2" h. $15, Coushatta reservation, 1986.

Twisted Handle

As the name implies, *twisted handle* is simply a handle that's been twisted. The handle could consist of several small pieces of reed or rattan, or it might be strips of cane. The twisted handle can easily be confused with a rope handle. Some baskets are found with a single twist; others, with a double twist.

Umbrella Stand

During the Victorian era, when the popularity of basketry was at its peak, the umbrella or *parasol* was an essential. Parasols weren't merely for rainy days, they were for any trips outside the house. Ladies of the day tried to avoid the sun as much as possible—a pale complexion was more desirable.

To accommodate the number of umbrellas in a home, umbrella stands were either bought or made. Some homes used hall trees along with umbrella stands, and the most popular stands were made like baskets. These were made in a variety of shapes and sizes, but most were made of wooden splints or willow.

Unfinished Basketry

Unfinished pieces of basketry have few uses, other than for study. In the Unity College basket display, unfinished baskets are used to show the steps in basketmaking. Oftentimes, pieces are found that can be finished, and if that's not feasible, the pieces of old splint can be used to repair broken baskets. Such splints will have aged enough to match those found on old baskets.

A pair of unfinished ash-splint and Hong Kong grass vases.

Two unfinished baskets in the Unity College display.

African violet in a basket.

Uses For Baskets

As always, baskets can be used for storing and carrying various items, but there are dozens of other uses as well.

Baskets can be lined with aluminum foil to make containers for small flowering plants; new or damaged baskets are best for this job. A basket of fruit or nuts makes a nice gift for a sick friend or shut-in, and a basket filled with talcum, soap, lotion, and a nice bathcloth or hand towel makes a welcome gift for someone in the hospital. Try a different approach to gift-giving and send a basket sometime, rather than flowers.

Small baskets can be used in numerous ways around the house, which allows one to show off a collection of baskets while keeping them useful. Baskets make great napkin or flatware holders for picnic tables, and they make excellent holders for mail and cosmetics.

One of the most enjoyable ways to use small covered baskets (new ones will work just as well as old) is for saving flower petals. Place the petals in a basket and add a few drops of your favorite perfume—the fragrance will linger for weeks. More perfume added at intervals revives the fragrance.

Vases With Basketry Covers

Basketmakers of the Northeast have been weaving covers on vases for nearly a century, and it's amazing how they're able to recognize each other's work still—their later work, that is.

The vase with the small top (left) was found at a yard sale in Portland, Maine. Later, while attending a basketry class conducted on the Penobscot Indian Reservation in Old Town, Maine, approximately 100 miles away, the vase was shown to the instructor—an older, very skilled Penobscot basketmaker. She immediately recognized the work as that of her sister-in-law from the 1930s. The cover is woven of thin strips of ash mixed with Hong Kong and sweet grass. The strips were originally dyed in shades of red and blue, but are now faded. The scalloped top of a red depression-glass vase can be seen at the top. The other vase is clear and about the same age, and the basketry cover is about the same.

Basketry-covered red vase. 6" dia, 9" h. $10, yard sale, 1986.

Basketry-covered clear vase. 6" dia, 10" h. $16, Topsham, Maine auction, 1987.

Vietnamese Baskets

Once basketmakers learn their craft, it isn't easy to change. The displaced Vietnamese coming into the United States are not changing their style of basketry as much as they're having to change the types of materials they use. They must either substitute their usual materials with American-grown cane, or try to have materials imported from home. Not all Vietnamese are making baskets here, but several are making them to be sold in gift shops. The Vietnamese-made baskets that were seen, were well made and very attractive.

New Vietnamese basket. 4" w, 6" l, 10" o.h. $15, New England gift shop, 1986.

Chitimacha cane wall basket, private collection, NPA.

Virginia Creeper

Virginia creeper, a vine, was used rather extensively in baskets about a century ago. It is also called *American ivy* and *five-leaf ivy* in some areas.

The most desirable runners, at that time, were those that grew close to the ground. The runners are brown and a bit rough, which gives the basket an almost antique appearance when new.

Virginia creeper is also called *woodbine,* and is sometimes mistaken for poison ivy. However, it has a five-part leaf, and poison ivy has only a three-part leaf. At one time, Virginia creeper was a highly cultivated plant because it was so pretty when the foliage turned scarlet in the fall. It has a small, round, dark-blue berry (that isn't edible), and it grows in the woods from Quebec to Florida, and around Texas and Mexico.

New Choctaw cane basket. 6" l, 9" o.h. $12, Choctaw reservation, 1986.

Wide-splint cane wall basket, lacquered. 6" w, 10" h. $10, Alabama antique shop, 1986.

Oak-splint wall basket, private collection, NPA.

Wall Baskets

Wall baskets were made by most basketmakers in all areas, for both their own use and for sale. They were used in a variety of ways, and their names often reflected their use. Wall baskets were used to hold knives and forks in some areas, combs and brushes in others, and in some places they were used to hold mail. In still other places they were filled with shuttles for the loom. Some had single pockets; others had two and three pockets. In the South, wall baskets were made of swamp cane; in the East, ash splint; and in Tennessee, Kentucky, Missouri, Kansas, and other areas, they were made of oak splints.

Wallet

This is a simple envelope-type wallet made of woven grass, and little is known about it. It appears to date around the 1920s or 1930s, and it is definately a souvenir-type basketry. This wallet resembles the palm-leaf purses made for women, but appears to be of a finely cut grass. A two-row design is worked in, on both the inside and outside pieces, and the edge is beautifully finished.

Woven grass wallet. 4½" X 4½" closed. $23, Maine antique shop, 1987.

Walnut

Lumber from the walnut tree has always been sought for making good furniture, but as far as is known, few, if any, walnut splints were used in basketry. The bark, however, was used for both splints and dye. Darker than the white oak splints often used with it, the inner bark of the walnut tree was split and used to make contrasting designs.

Waste Baskets

Waste baskets are modern basketry items and weren't even known or used as such until around the turn of the twentieth century. Prior to that time, baskets were used for saving papers like receipts, letters, and bills, and they were used as plunder baskets—but they were not used for collecting trash.

Shortly after the turn of the century, imported Oriental baskets began to be used for holding excess or waste papers; thus, the waste basket was born. In recent years, basketmakers have recognized the need for waste baskets and have begun making them. At a showing of Coushatta Indian-made pine needle baskets a few years ago, there were five different sizes of waste baskets on display.

New Choctaw cane waste basket. 15" dia, 16" h. $50, Choctaw reservation, 1986.

Waterproof Baskets

A couple of centuries ago—in some areas only a century ago—when there were no plastic containers or wooden buckets, ways had to be devised for carrying water from springs and creeks. This was especially true for the people of the arid sections of the Southwest.

The Apaches are credited with making the first woven water jugs—they were the most skilled basketmakers—but it's believed that the Paiutes made the best waterproof jugs. Their jugs were made of willow coated with gum from the pinon trees. The Havasupais are credited with making the first stand-up basketry water jugs—those with pointed bottoms made for standing in the ground. The Cherokees also made waterproof baskets of double-woven river cane coated with bees wax.

Weavers

Whether they're made of wood splints, swamp cane, or bamboo, the pieces used in over and under weaving around the sides of a woven basket are called weavers. Even the braided and plaited sweet grass used with ash splints are called weavers when used to weave the sides of a basket.

Wedge

The wedge is another tool necessary in the preparation of splint basketry materials, especially oak, elm, and hickory splints. The wedge is inserted into logs or sections of a tree, and when it is hit with a maul, it breaks the sections apart.

Wheel Covers

When a carriage or wagon was used to transport the family to church on Sunday, or when a lady traveled any place, she wore long, billowing dresses with at least a half dozen ruffled petticoats, and sometimes she would wear a hoop skirt. Whether a hoop skirt or petticoat, entering or leaving the carriage was difficult. This was especially true during winter and on rainy days.

Most ladies had very few pieces of clothing, and took very good care of what they did have. Eventually, woven wheel covers were invented, which served to cover the mud as passengers entered and left their vehicles. Later, wheel covers were offered in catalogues as "French wicker wheel covers and dress guards."

Some of these covers were destroyed when they were on the wheels, and others were discarded when they were no longer needed, and were eventually destroyed. Those that weren't destroyed simply rotted away in the weather. They are scarce now and cost in the $150 bracket when found.

Wickerwork

Many baskets are described as wicker baskets, yet the dictionary describes wickerwork as "thin, flexible twigs woven together."

Actually, *wickerwork* means that the *spokes* or *vertical* part of a basket is more rigid than the weavers. To further confuse the issue, some of the old basketry instruction books referred to a number of weaves as *wicker weaves*. These included the simple over-and-under weave and the double over-and-under weave, where two weavers were used as one. There was also a triple weave.

Willow wickerwork covered carrying basket. 14" w, 17" l, 19" o.h. $75, Florida antique shop.

Old basketmakers used dozens of different weaves, including one called a *Japanese weave* in which a single weaver was passed in front of two spokes and behind a third, using three spokes in one weave. This was often called *wickerwork*.

Wicopy

Wicopy is a modernization of the old term *kakisooikbe*, used by the Penobscots for a century or more to describe their ash-splint basket materials. It has also been called *wigobi*. All three terms were used to describe the flexibility of ash splints, which can be twisted and turned in various ways without breaking.

*Old willow basket with crisscross handles on the sides. 12" dia, 9½" h. **$55**, Ohio antique shop, 1986.*

*Willow basket that may be part of a nesting set. 14" dia, 4" h. **$20**, Maine auction, 1986.*

*Willow basket with coats of white paint on the bottom and red paint around the sides. 16" dia, 5" h. **$20**, Maine auction, 1986.*

Willow

Through the years, willow trees have served us well. In earlier years, willow trees were unequalled for holding unruly streams. More useful, perhaps, were the branches or *osiers* used for making wiers, cradles, baskets, and finally, wicker furniture.

Despite its many uses, willow was not cultivated during the early years; instead, it was allowed to grow wherever plants sprouted—unless they interfered with housebuilding, gardening, or farming. Then, with the popularity of wicker furniture shortly before the turn of the century, Americans began to see the value of growing and harvesting willow holts.

Prior to that time, most willow had been imported from England, Belgium, Holland, and Germany—Germany being the leader with a reported 50,000 acres of willows planted in 1898.

At about the same time, wicker furniture production and willow basketry began to skyrocket. The need for domestic willow became apparent, and so the Department of Agriculture began to educate the farmers in the ways of growing willow for profit. Free instructions were offered for planting, growing, and harvesting willow, and different varieties were recommended for certain areas.

Green willow was highly recommended for the southern states of Alabama, Mississippi, and Louisiana, and for some of the northern states. Purple willow was recommended for any area where willow would grow, and was one of the best varieties of willow around—it could be planted in rows, making it easier to cultivate with horse-drawn plows. Lemley willow was especially recommended for planting in Ohio, Indiana and Maryland, but could be grown any place. It was least likely to become diseased, and therefore, was most highly recommended. The willow holts grew fast and sold for good money, but there was still enough left over for basketmakers.

Due to its lightness and strength, willow is accorded a distinct place in the history of basketry. It has been used since the beginning of time. The Romans are known to have used willow for making baskets and bee hives, as well as fences for their gardens. For years in Europe, willow was held in such high esteem that even in Pliny's time, he wrote, "Cato held an osier bed in higher estimation than an olive plantation or than wheat or meadow land."

The beauty of willow was not overlooked then, nor is it now. The white satiny smoothness of it's new branches gives it added appeal, while the brown of aged baskets gives it an added dimension. Willow baskets were so attractive that bakers once used them in their windows for displaying their finest pastries.

Not all willow branches were used in the sizes gathered from the tree. Many chose large branches or osiers for certain baskets, and smaller ones for other sizes. There were also the basketmakers, some Indian tribes among them, who opted for splitting willow branches into three pieces for very fine weaving. To split them, the branches were first soaked well, and then cut diagonally across one end. Using the Indian method of hands and teeth, the branch was divided into three parts by keeping one part between the teeth and holding the other two parts in each hand. The branch was pulled downward and outward until it came apart.

Winnowing Basket

The white man used a winnowing basket more for separating chaff from grain, dirt from seeds, and a few other chores. The western Indians used it for dirt, chaff, and leaves from edible nuts picked up in the forest. In the South it was used for winnowing corn, rice, and other foods. The old winnowing baskets made by some of the western tribes are more interesting because they were used both for winnowing and cooking. This eliminated some work as hot coals were placed in the basket after the nuts were gathered. In some instances,

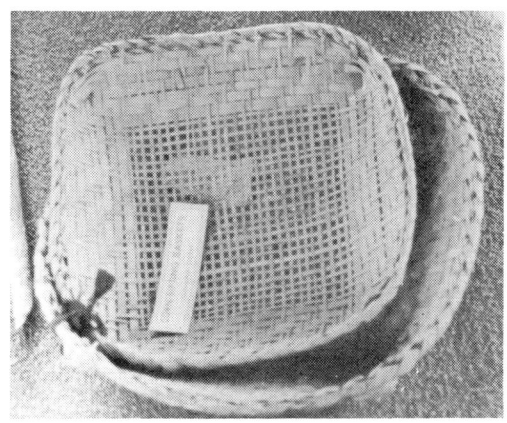

Late cane-winnowing or corn-sifting baskets, Miccosukee Reservation Museum, NPA.

the tray was agitated as the nuts cooked—the nuts winnowed and cooked at the same time. Roasted or parched nuts could be preserved longer than fresh ones.

Large basket, 14" dia, 10½" h, $23, Maine antique shop, 1987. Small basket, 6¼" dia, 4¼" h, $5, Tennessee flea market, 1986.

Wire Baskets

Not all old baskets were woven, coiled, or twined out of native materials—some were factory-made of wire. Since the factory-made wire baskets are becoming more common at antique shows, shops, and malls, they are included here. In antique places, these baskets are called by various names, such as potato, egg, or apple baskets. They were used in some of the old general stores to display fruit, eggs, and potatoes.

181

Wire Grass

Wire grass is one of a variety of grasses that grows over much of the United States, and at one time grew so abundantly in southeast Alabama that the county seat of Houston became known as "the Hub of the Wiregrass," a name it retains to this day. Around 1900, the newspaper in Dothan Alabama (the county seat) was called The Wiregrass Siftings.

Wiregrass is a tall plant growing to heights of three to four feet. It grows wild in the lowlands, especially the sandy lowlands of the South. It also grows in certain marshy areas. Although little information could be found on the use of wiregrass in the Deep South, it is known to have been quite popular during the turn-of-the-century basketry revival when it could be bought in the same stores that sold reed and rattan.

Wisteria vine and Hong Kong grass basket. 10" dia, 5" h. $17.50, Maine antique show. 1986.

Wisteria Vine

Wisteria is a woody-looking vine of the pea family named for Caspar Wistar (1761–1818), an American anatomist. It grows best in the southern and eastern states. Most of the flowers are purple or white and look like large bunches of grapes. In the South, the plant is cultivated, but when new growth starts on the trees, it can cover them in a short amount of time. The wisteria vine is a fast growing plant, which makes it a natural for basketmakers. The vines can be used in either their natural state or peeled. Peeling is easy if a knife is run down one side of the vine. When the bark is left on, its grayish-green color gives the basket an instant antique appearance. Wisteria was often mixed with grape and honeysuckle vines to make baskets.

Wooden-Bottomed Baskets

Many baskets will be found with wooden bottoms. Some are new ones coming in from as far away as Bangladesh, but a large number of older baskets have wooden bottoms, including the Nantucket Lightship baskets. When basketry experienced its revival in the 1950s, many beginners preferred making baskets, serving trays, and other basketry items on a wooden base. This was easier, as holes were bored into the plywood and the spokes fastened easily. This way, the spokes and weavers became one and the same. See Fifties Baskets.

Beautifully woven, old-oak splint half-bushel farm or work basket, private collection, NPA.

Large swing-handle farm basket. 18" dia, 13" h. $225, Maine auction, 1987.

Open work basket of ash splint. 9½" dia, 5" o.h. $25, Maine antique show, 1987.

Work Basket, Open

This is a work basket of the sewing variety. It was more popular during earlier years, but some were made well into the tourist-trade years. Some are plain, so they can be used for other purposes, while many have the small baskets or pockets inside so they can be used as fitted sewing baskets. Without the pockets, they make excellent scrap baskets, or baskets to hold knitting and crochet threads.

Ash-splint swing-handle basket, damaged. $150, Maine auction, 1987.

Work Baskets

The term *work basket* is applied to two entirely different types of baskets. One is the work, burden, or farm basket—the type a farmer would use in his work. The other type is a sewing basket, usually an open one. In some parts of the country, the terms *sewing basket* and *work basket* are interchangeable.

Basket made of finely split oak splints. 9" dia, 9" o.h. $250, North Carolina antique shop, 1986.

183

Covered basket woven of wide and narrow ash splints. 13" dia, 11" h. $75, Massachusetts antique mall, 1986.

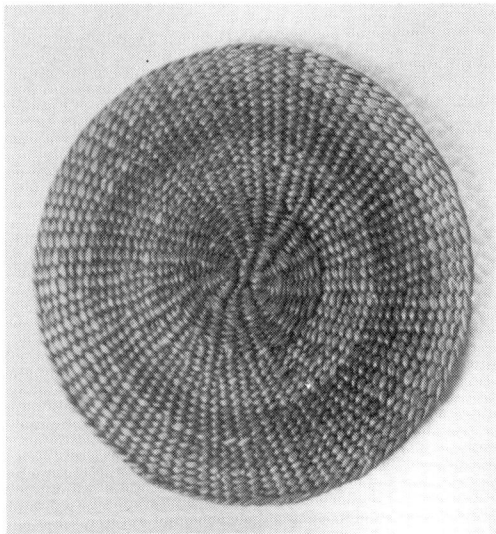

Miniature twined mat. 3" dia. $28, Vermont mall, 1986.

Woven Baskets

Actually, there are only two basic methods of basketry—weaving and coiling. The mystery, intrigue, and beauty of baskets comes from the many different ways of weaving and coiling. Twining is an example: It is basically weaving but with a flair, such as twisting two very small, flexible weavers together between each spoke. Different types of weaves may be used.

Wrapped Handle

The biggest difference between the rope and the wrapped handle is that the wrapped handle usually has more than one rod in its foundation, and it is wrapped solidly from one end to the other. Also, wrapped handles are fancier. Some of the old basketmakers often put a wooden rod, like a small handle, on the bottom of the wrapped handle, and then wrapped it to give it a three-prong effect. This was called a *bracing rod.*

X-Binding

An *X-binding* on a basket is the same as a double-wrapped rim, but this name is used more often because it's more descriptive. See Double-Wrapped Rim.

Tall yarn basket of ash splints, sweet grass, and Hong Kong grass, 8" dia, 10" h, $45, Maine antique show, 1987; shorter basket, same materials, 8" dia, 6" h, $40, Maine antique show, 1987.

Yarn Basket

A few years ago, no picture of a country home was complete without a basket full of yarn on the floor, or on a table near a comfortable rocker. That homey scene is still used today, but the baskets used in most of the pictures were made for another purpose—usually they were candy baskets.

Basketmakers of the Northeast made baskets specifically for yarn because so many people in the area knitted. Ladies seldom went any place without bringing along their knitting—they continuously knitted warm clothing for the cold winters. Yarn baskets came in different sizes to accommodate the needs of the knitter, no doubt. The handle could be slipped over her arm so she could take out the yarn without difficulty. The majority of the baskets were made of ash splints and sweet grass, but some can be found with the addition of Hong Kong grass.

Yellow Dye

Yellow dye could be made from several materials, including woodchips from the *fustic* tree. Some basketmakers used yellow root or sumac, it all depended on where the person lived. In the Northeast, they used the roots of *gold-thread* (coptis trifolia), an evergreen plant whose yellow roots were also used in medicine. The dye made from gold-thread was strong, clear, brilliant, and long lasting. In Louisiana and other parts of the South, basketmakers used a plant called *butterweed*, which grows wild, to make yellow dye.

Yellow Root

Both mountaineer and Cherokee basketmakers have long used the roots of a plant called *yellow root* to make yellow dye for the oak splints and cane used in their basketry.

Yew

Yew is an evergreen related to both pine and hemlock, which probably explains why it was used so much in basketry years ago. The bark was used more than the wood, although the wood was close-grained and elastic when split into flexible flat weavers.

Old yucca-wrapped tray, Lightner Museum collection, NPA.

Yucca

Yucca is a plant of the lily family that grows abundantly in the arid Southwest. It has stiff, sword-shaped leaves that are used extensively by the Indians living in the area. They prefer the *plains* and the *banana* yucca. The leaves of the banana yucca are split and used as strips to make plaited or twilled baskets, while bundles of leaves may be used as a foundation for coiled baskets. The leaves are a delicate, natural shade, and the red roots can be used to make designs.

Plains yucca has a yellowish-green leaf that can be split and used the same as banana yucca. When cut narrow enough, the yucca strips resemble raffia and can be used the same way as raffia. Yucca leaves can be gathered any time of the year and used green, or they can be wrapped in a moist towel and kept in a damp place until needed. Yucca can be used much as the Afro-American or Gullah people of South Carolina use palmetto, who have recently taken advantage of modern appliances and now freeze the palmetto before using it. They say this method makes the palmetto last longer and work more easily.

Zoar Community

In 1817, a group of approximately 400 people, who called themselves the Separatist Society of Zoar, migrated to America from Wurttemberg, Germany. They came to escape persecution for their religious beliefs, and found friends among the Quakers, who welcomed them and helped establish their settlement in Ohio. For the next 13 years, the community prospered and gained new members. Membership finally reached 500.

Little changed for them during the next 20 years—they continued farming and making baskets. When the leader, Baumeler, died in 1853, the community began to decline, and by 1898, its communistic features had been abolished. Like many other societies in America, they are known to have made and sold baskets of many types, but none have been found that could be authenticated.

Nesting set of seven new baskets. 3" to 14" dia. $1,995, from the maker, 1987.

Zeh, Stephen

Stephen Zeh (pronounced ZA) is a contemporary Temple, Maine basketmaker who is striving to make baskets as well, or better than, other old-time New England basketmakers. He makes a beautiful brown-ash swing-handle in singles and nesting sets of seven.